the autobiography
of baseball

Hank Aaron Grover Cleveland Alexander C

Ashburn Ernie Banks Cool Papa Bell Johnn

Bottomley Lou Boudreau George Brett Lou

Campanella Rod Carew Max Carey Steve Car

Jack Chesbro Fred Clarke Roberto Clemen

Conigliaro Sam Crawford Candy Cummin

Delahanty Bill Dickey Joe DiMaggio Larry

Red Faber Bob Feller Rollie Fingers White

Charlie Gehringer Bob Gibson Kid Gleason H

Lefty Grove Tony Gwynn Gabby Hartnet

Hernandez Harry Hooper Rogers Hornsby C

Jackson Judy Johnson Walter Johnson Al

Killebrew Sandy Koufax Napoleon Lajoie

Maranville Juan Marichal Roger Maris Rut

Willie Mays Dan McGann Joe McGinnity

Musial Hal Newhouser Kid Nichols Phil N

Gaylord Perry Eddie Plank Kirby Puckett Sa

Robinson Jackie Robinson Edd Roush Babe

Mike Schmidt Tom Seaver Joe Sewell Ozz

Speaker Willie Stargell Casey Stengel Frank

Paul Waner Zack Wheat Doc White Hoyt Wi

Anson   Luis Aparicio   Luke Appling   Richie

the autobiography of baseball

the inside story from the stars who played the game

Bill Dahlen   Jake Daubert   Dizzy Dean   Ed
y Leo Durocher   Jimmy Dykes   Johnny Evers
ord   Jimmy Foxx   Frank Frisch   Lou Gehrig
k Greenberg   Ken Griffey, Jr.   Burleigh Grimes
Harry Heilmann   Rickey Henderson   Keith
l Hubbell   Monte Irvin   Travis Jackson   Reggie
ine   Willie Keeler   Mike King Kelly   Harmon
op Lloyd   Al Lopez   Mickey Mantle   Rabbit
Marquard   Christy Mathewson   Don Mattingly
n McGraw   Johnny Mize   Joe M   **by joseph wallace**
o Satchel Paige   Jim Palmer   Herb Pennock   **foreword by ira berkow**
Rice   Cal Ripken, Jr.   Brooks Rob
uth   Nolan Ryan   Ryne Sandberg   Ray Schalk
Smith   Warren Spahn   **harry n. abrams, inc., publishers**
omas   Pie Traynor   Honus Wagner   Ed Walsh
m   Ted Williams   Smoky Joe Wood   Cy Young

For Sharon, Shana, and Jacob, all-stars

Editor: Sharon AvRutick
Designer: Judith Michael
Photo Editor: John K. Crowley

Page 1:
Mickey Mantle, the most
prodigious switch-hitter
in baseball history.

Pages 4–5:
Kids and their baseball heroes
(here, Joe DiMaggio in 1948)
have always had a special bond.

Library of Congress
Cataloging-in-Publication Data

Wallace, Joseph E.
The autobiography of baseball : the inside story
from the stars who played the game / Joseph
Wallace.
p.   cm.
Includes bibliographical references
(p.) and index.
ISBN 0–8109–1925–7 (hardcover)
1. Baseball—United States—History.
2. Baseball players—United States—
Anecdotes.   I. Title.
GV863.A1W355   1998
796.357′092′273—dc21   98–12729

Printed and bound in Japan

Harry N. Abrams, Inc.
100 Fifth Avenue
New York, N.Y. 10011
www.abramsbooks.com

contents

foreword

It was a late, luscious morning in March 1970 in Pompano, Florida, when white baseballs were batted so high into the perfect blue sky that they momentarily appeared like stars, when the chatter in the infield was as cheerful as songbirds, and when the dreams of all those in their team uniform were as sweet as the small, sun-dappled ballpark. It was spring training, that exquisite time of year, a time one wishes could last forever.

It doesn't, of course. For baseball, though, in which the beginning of each new season brings a sense of hope, a sense of rebirth, a sense of unbounded possibilities, spring training begins what is indeed the Autobiography of a Baseball Season. And on that morning in March 1970, I had occasion, as a sports columnist, to sit with Ted Williams, then the manager of the Washington Senators.

Williams was called "The Splendid Splinter" in his playing days, days that were extraordinary, culminating perhaps in 1941 when he batted .406, the last man to bat .400 or over in the major leagues. And while he was still splendid, he was not quite a splinter any longer. In fact, even on this warm day, he self-consciously wore his windbreaker to cover his stomach.

We talked on a wide range of topics regarding baseball. And then I asked him, "Is it true that you were such a great hitter because of your exceptional eyesight and reflexes?" Williams was supposed to have been able to read a car's license plate from a block away, and it was said that tests he took as a pilot in the Air Force demonstrated uncommon motor skills.

Williams, still imposing, and in that John Wayne voice, turned to the then-young sportswriter, and said in a pedagogical but decidedly emphatic manner, "That's bunk!" (or a word to that effect). "It was trial and damn error, trial and damn error, trial and damn error, trial and damn error!"

Despite what the wondrous Williams said, I believed it was both—great natural talent combined with great work ethic. And after reading this insightful and entertaining book, *The Autobiography of Baseball*, I am convinced of it.

There is Satchel Paige talking about being the best brick thrower in his neighborhood on the south side of Mobile, Alabama. "I didn't learn to be a brick thrower," he said. "It was born in me. A musician is born with music. A pitcher is born a pitcher." And there is Sandy Koufax: "Something in my arm is built a little different."

But Koufax also explains how he went from what is known as a thrower to a pitcher, making the transition from just a wild .500 talent to a thinking-man's star professional. He had learned after several seasons to control his emotions—and his fast ball. He realized that he could still throw hard but without pressing, which meant "taking the grunt out of it."

There is Ty Cobb figuring out the best way to slide when stealing a base ("look in the eyes of the fielder, to know where the ball is coming") to Rogers Hornsby's belief that thinking too much when in a slump only compounds it—he'd try one or two small changes in his swing and then "try to think of something else" unrelated to baseball.

And there is the psychological motivation, such as that of Zack Wheat: "I developed a contempt for pitchers." Or Bob Gibson, who even when he was playing in an All-Star Game wouldn't be friendly to his teammates because, he said, two days later, they'd be the enemy again and "trying to beat my brains out." "I always felt—and still feel today—that when people don't know anything about you they have a tendency to fear you."

And the little tricks, such as Leo Durocher telling Willie Mays to pull his pants up so that they would shorten the strike zone for him. And general conditioning: "The arm is only as good as the legs," said pitcher Warren Spahn.

And while it often seems so easy for major leaguers, many, if not all, suffer from some form of stress at one time or another, from trying to make the team to crucial moments in big games (when Walter Johnson, near the end of his glorious career with Washington, was called on in relief in the ninth inning of the seventh game of the 1924 World Series, he recalled: "If I didn't actually pray, I sort of was thinking along those lines"). And when Chief Bender, the Hall of Fame pitcher for Connie Mack's old A's, retired, he said the stress continued, and he got thinner and thinner because the acid in his stomach "made it impossible to eat."

Yet dreams remain a huge part of the success of anyone, particularly the athlete, who, as Roy Campanella once said, must have a lot of little boy in him. "I remember some of the day dreams I had at St. Mary's [his childhood boarding school]," recalled Babe Ruth, "and how far off they seemed and unlikely, and still came true. . . ."

The racial and ethnic prejudice that exists to varying degrees in the rest of society have been experienced on baseball fields by, among others, Italians and Jews and blacks. "If prejudice does exist," Hank Greenberg wrote to a Jewish youngster, "then let it spur you on to greater achievement rather than accept it and be licked by it."

But, in the words of our finest ballplayers, as combined gracefully in this book by Joseph Wallace, and in the accompanying photographs, we are also treated to a history of a nation's myths as embodied in baseball—and the inevitable reality, which is sometimes happy, sometimes painful.

But then it is springtime again. The sun is warm, the breeze is choice, the players sweat. And white baseballs soar in the blue morning sky like so many stars, like so many hopes, like so many dreams.

Ira Berkow

"Scallions are the greatest cure for a batting slump ever invented."
—Babe Ruth

I love listening to baseball players talk about their game. I love it when they relax, grow thoughtful, move past the clichés, and discuss why they have devoted their lives to baseball. I find myself enthralled by the chance to hear how they approach their craft, what challenges they've overcome to succeed in this most difficult of all sports, and—inevitably—how they face their declining skills and the realization that their exciting, fulfilling, and lucrative careers are coming to an end.

In gathering material for *The Baseball Anthology*, my previous baseball book, I kept unearthing fascinating, long-forgotten interviews with the game's superstars. Since that project focused more on writers' views of baseball history, I was able to include only a couple of the interviews. But then, after the book was published, I found that many readers were especially taken with the autobiographical segments, and it was clear what my next project would be.

Therefore, with the exception of my own introductory and linking passages, the players speak for themselves in *The Autobiography of Baseball*. Who better to tell us about a ballplayer's career than the ballplayer himself?

The Autobiography of Baseball is, in a sense, an oral history, but not like any other. Readers will not find the complete life story of any single player here. Instead, I have interwoven the reminiscences of more than 150 Hall of Fame, future Hall of Fame, and near–Hall of Fame ballplayers from more than a century's worth of radio and television shows, newspaper and magazine articles, books, and never-before-published taped interviews. I've included countless revealing quotes, telling insights, and sometimes outrageous tales that allow great players from throughout the game's history to give us an unparalleled inside look at the arc, the shape, the highs and lows of a major-league career.

What you will find here is, in effect, an extended conversation among superstars from every era—as it would have been if somehow all these men had gathered in a single room and just talked baseball:

Opposite:
Roy Campanella, for years the dominant catcher in the National League.

- Carl Hubbell, Lefty Grove, and Frank Thomas recall the long road to the major leagues.
- Babe Ruth and Tony Gwynn discuss the best way to hold the bat while swinging, while Harry Heilmann and Ted Williams add their views on proper bat weight.
- Satchel Paige, Juan Marichal, Christy Mathewson, and Steve Carlton compare the relative merits of stones, bricks, and slingshots in helping a young boy master control of his pitches.
- Nap Lajoie and Johnny Bench give us glimpses inside the minds of great hitters trapped in agonizing slumps.
- Hank Greenberg, Jackie Robinson, and Roberto Clemente compare notes about overcoming racial prejudice to carve out a brilliant career.
- Tris Speaker and Willie Mays talk about chasing down fly balls.
- And Ty Cobb, Grover Cleveland Alexander, and Mike Schmidt discuss facing the end of their careers with dignity and equanimity.

In compiling their words I've tried to stand aside and let the game's superstars provide their surprising, intriguing, insightful, and irreplaceable perspectives about what makes baseball the richest, most complex, and most enjoyable game around. Putting *The Autobiography of Baseball* together, I felt privileged to have the chance to listen in.

I would never have been able to put this book together without the aid of many individuals. At the Baseball Hall of Fame in Cooperstown, New York, James Gates, Jr., Librarian of the National Baseball Library and Archive, opened the doors to me and invited me to stay as long as I liked. So I stuck around for a while, receiving priceless help—and welcome companionship—from Tim Wiles, Greg Harris, Lesley Humphreys, Bruce Markusen, and the rest of the library's research staff. Time and again, they pointed me in directions I never would have found on my own. I am especially grateful to Tim and Lori for making me feel as if I were a friend coming for a visit, not just a researcher bearing an endless list of requests.

Thanks also to the people of Cooperstown, who were incredibly friendly and never asked why I kept showing up on the streets of their beautiful town during blizzard conditions in midwinter, when the locals know enough to stay indoors. I'm grateful to the staff of the Lakefront Motel for keeping their establishment open even when I was the only guest on Super Bowl Sunday, and for always finding a quiet room for me when the motel was packed in midsummer. The Doubleday Café provided me with good food, much-appreciated glasses of Old Slugger ale, and a cheerful atmosphere after many a day I'd spent poring over illegible clippings. Thanks to Diana, Debbie, Carrie, Laura, Monica, Kelly, Barb, and everyone else there for making one tired and frequently grouchy lone diner always feel welcome.

At Abrams, I'm grateful to Paul Gottlieb (publisher) and Don Guerra (director of sales) for having faith in this concept and to Sharon AvRutick (editor), Judith Michael (designer), John Crowley (picture editor), Lauren Boucher (text permissions), and Richard Slovak (proofreader) for their dependably brilliant work. Every writer should have the chance to work with this team.

Opposite:
Ken Griffey, Jr., at the conclusion of another perfect swing. "See it—and hit it," he said simply.

10

Johnny Evers, the high-strung Hall of Fame se

illusions of a future in baseball, as he revealed

Troy, New York: "I was never much of a ballpl

particularly attacked with any fond hopes of be

I attended the Christian Brothers' School—I lea

on windows and fences—you know what I me

and was getting on nicely too, when I was tak

from the poisons in the paints. Well, one day a

on Labor Day, September 6, 1902. The Troy tea

tin' in the grandstand near the players' bench,

of the Troy team moaning the loss of his shortst

denly ill which left the team in a bad hole at th

and swearing at the state of affairs until somet

only know that I left my seat without a word to

bench, walked up to the manager, and told him

as substitute for the sick shortstop. That was

never even hoped to be a ballplayer before. Well,

way—I felt myself getting smaller than I alread

you will have to do." And Evers did, too, playin

to get his job back. Evers played regularly from

and skill that would distinguish his major-leag

nd baseman for the Cubs, was one who had no

a 1914 interview describing   in

r, and besides I was pretty li   ot

ning a great ball player. After finishing school—

ed the sign writer's trade—used to paint signs

. I was just setting on that for my life's trade,

sick with painters' colic, a disease contracted

r that I happened to attend a ball game. It was

was playing the Cuban Giants. So—I was a-set-

ching them practice, when I heard the manager

. It seemed that this player had been taken sud-

last moment. Well, sir, I heard them grumbling

ng happened to me—I could never describe it—I

ny one and vaulted over the rail to the players'

t I was a ball player and to put me in the game

stinct, I guess—I don't know what else. I had

e manager looked me over in a surprised sort of

was—and then said: "Get in a suit, kid; I guess

well enough that the sick player was never able

at first game, hitting and fielding with the fire

career—a career that was to begin quite soon.

RESERVOIR OVAL
100 LB TEAM
WINNERS OF THE NEW YORK
CITY PLAYGROUND
CHAMPIONSHIP 1916.

More Than a Game

When we were children, so many of us lived for baseball. We spent hours each summer day bouncing a pink rubber ball—a "spaldeen"—off a stoop, chasing down long flies in a local sandlot game, or throwing a hardball back and forth endlessly. We'd play in schoolyards, on fields, or in alleys. We'd dream about baseball at night. And always, we imagined that we were major-league stars surrounded by a ghost team of our favorite players. A long hit, a great play, or even just the *thwock* of the ball into the glove could allow us to pretend, however briefly, that we'd helped our team win the World Series.

"We'd play stickball in the streets, and every once in a while, on a Sunday, there'd be a few cars and it added to the enjoyment and excitement of the game to catch a ball and avoid being run down by an irate motorist," Hank Greenberg wrote of his Bronx childhood in *Hank Greenberg: The Story of My Life* (1989). "They'd blow their horns and jam on the brakes, but the kids didn't pay much attention. The game was more important."

With these simple words recalling a distant time, Greenberg, whose hitting prowess for the Detroit Tigers would carry him to the Hall of Fame, spoke for many of us. But from this shared childhood fascination emerged two distinct paths: Greenberg and other future superstars chose to pursue the pipe dream of a baseball career, while most of us put aside any realistic hope of making

"My closest buddies were my teammates," said Hank Greenberg, here striking a basketball pose while at James Monroe High School in the Bronx, New York, in 1929.

Left:
"In public school, athletics occupied about 85 percent of my mind and time," recalled Hank Greenberg (back row, third from left).

Opposite:
Portrait of Lou Gehrig (seated, second from right) as a young man. "I have a medal at home given me in recognition of my work as a catcher—a left-handed catcher, mind you—which helped to win the 100-pound championship for the Reservoir Ovals team" in New York City, Gehrig recalled in 1930.

the majors soon after we played our first pick-up game. At what point did Greenberg's potential—and that of other superstars—become clear? How did their special talent for the game begin to show itself?

Examine the words of future stars, and you'll see that—even as children— these players were different. Almost from the start, many showed a passion for competition, almost an obsessiveness, that dwarfed anything displayed by the rest of us. No matter the circumstances, these boys had to be competing. Here's Ted Williams on his childhood in San Diego, from *My Turn At Bat* (1969):

Play, play, play, play. Horseshoes, handball, a game called "Big League," where all it took was two guys, a bat and one of those ten-inch softballs with the high seams. With those seams you could make the ball do anything— curve, drop, screwball, knuckleball—and we'd play against the backstop of a softball field, where there was a screen with a bar across the middle. If you hit above the bar it was a triple, below it was a double. A groundball past the pitcher was a single. Hit the bar and if the other guy didn't catch it coming off it was a home run. We'd play Big League by the hour.

In *My Life Is Baseball* (1968), Hall of Famer Frank Robinson remembered his childhood in a very similar way. "My life in those days, as it is now, was made of unequal parts that all spelled b-a-s-e-b-a-l-l—baseball, from morning to night," Robinson wrote, continuing:

Ask my mother. I'd go out early in the morning, maybe come home for lunch, then stay out till seven, eight, nine, ten at night, until it got dark. I'd come racing home with the moon and go to the oven and pull out whatever was left for me to eat. Mom would be waiting, and chiding, "Why do you want to be out so late?"
"Playing ball."
She'd sigh. "It's too dark to see."

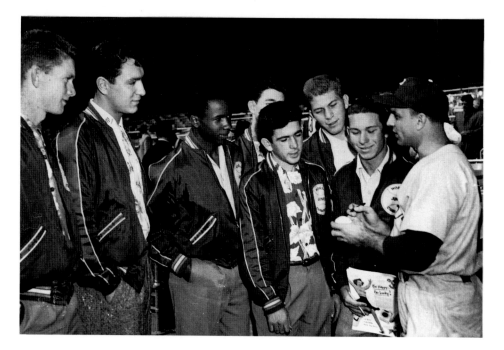

Frank Robinson (center), as a fifteen-year-old getting Phillie catcher Andy Seminick's autograph at the 1950 World Series. "My life in those days, as it is now, was made of unequal parts that all spelled b-a-s-e-b-a-l-l," he wrote during his Hall of Fame career.

"Mom," I'd say, "we played until we couldn't see at all." As if she didn't understand.

Later, when I got a little older, she kept after me to go to work. But I couldn't see it. I said, "Ma, I don't want to work. I want to play ball."

When there was no game available, budding stars found other ways to improve their skills. Even at an early age, many of those destined to be Hall of Fame pitchers began to focus on improving the accuracy of their powerful arms. "Around the farm I was always throwing things and usually throwing at something else," Philadelphia Phillies superstar Grover Cleveland Alexander told *The New York World* about his childhood in Elba, Nebraska. "I was continually being scolded by my mother for coming home with holes in my pockets worn by rocks."

Christy Mathewson, famed for his pinpoint control during his Hall of Fame career with the New York Giants, had specific targets for his powerful throws. "When I was nine years old, I could throw a stone farther than any of the boys who were my chums," he recalled in a 1912 article in *St. Nicholas Magazine*. "Then I used to go out in the woods and throw at squirrels and blackbirds, and even sparrows; and many a bag full of game I got with stones."

Decades later, Steve Carlton, the dominant National League left-hander of the 1970s, followed the same path. "We used to hunt with rocks," he told *The Sporting News* in 1977. "I used to knock doves off the telephone wires. I was about 12 or 13 then. I figured everybody could hit birds throwing stones. I didn't think my arm was unusual."

The Giants' 1960s superstar Juan Marichal employed an even more innovative method of improving his accuracy, as he related in *A Pitcher's Story* (1967):

In a crazy way—one that may not make sense—I learned "control"—by using a slingshot! To me, a slingshot was almost a piece of baseball equipment. I would sling a rock against a tree, or throw a baseball against the same tree,

Destined for stardom from the moment he found he could knock small birds and animals out of a tree with a well-aimed rock, Christy Mathewson (back row, second from right) graduated to throwing a ball over a plate by the time he reached college.

and the two were very much the same, to me. This does not mean I advise youngsters to use slingshots for baseball practice. And it does not mean I invented a new special way to practice control, because to begin with the basic purpose of the slingshot was to hurt birds.

Birds and animals were not the only targets of future Hall of Fame pitchers' strong, accurate arms. Satchel Paige, perhaps the greatest of all Negro League pitchers—and a star as well for the major-league Cleveland Indians at the end of his career—always claimed that he built up his arm strength throwing at another type of target. The following is from *Pitchin' Man* (1948):

We had a pretty rough gang down on the South Side of Mobile [Alabama], near the Bay, where I was born and raised.

We were exclusive, that's the word. When the South Side gave a picnic, the North Side couldn't come. They always tried, for sure. But we chased them right back.

Fact is we stoned them back—with bricks. We had the best sham battlin' crew in Mobile Bay and I was known as the straightest brick thrower in Mobile.

Y'understand now, I didn't learn to be a brick thrower. It was born in me.

A musician is born with music. A pitcher is born a pitcher. He's born with his best pitch. . . .

I was born with speed and control. I came into the world with both right from the start. 'Course I didn't realize I had a gift till I began to pitch professional baseball, but I shoulda known early.

I shoulda known when I throwed my first brick.

Just as future pitchers tend to focus on their throwing arms, Hall of Fame hitters become obsessed with their reflexes and batting eye at an age when most of us would be content to hit a Wiffle ball with authority. "All I ever did since I was six was play ball—except for when I was in the Army and one other time," Willie Mays told *This Week Magazine* in 1954. "That was when I was 15, eight years ago. I got a job in a cafe in Birmingham. I washed dishes. Folks there treated me grade-A. But you know how long I lasted? Just one week— then I quit. Now, I ask you, how're you going to concentrate on cafe work when all the time your mind is swinging a bat?"

Joe Sewell, Hall of Fame shortstop and third baseman with the Indians and Yanks in the 1920s and early 1930s, was equally entranced by hitting. "I can't ever remember a time when I was a boy back in Titus [Alabama] when I couldn't throw up a Coca-Cola top or a rock and not hit it with a broomstick handle or a stick," said Sewell, who would typically strike out fewer than ten times a season during his major-league career. "All that time I was developing my reflexes, my coordination, and I've always had good eyes."

Invaluable lessons could come from surprising places, as Eddie Mathews, third baseman with the Braves in the 1950s and 1960s, revealed in his 1978 induction to the Hall of Fame. "[My father] and my mother got me started," Mathews recalled. "She used to pitch to me and my dad would shag and as I got older, every time I hit a ball back through the middle, close to my mother, I got

18

Willie Mays called his first autobiography Born to Play Ball—*and even after he became a major-league superstar, he would still take to the New York City streets for a pick-up stickball game.*

Joe Sewell's effortless, efficient swing was the result of good eyes and endless hours of childhood practice.

Opposite:
"All I ever did since I was six was play ball," Willie Mays said. While he was still in his teens, Mays was already starring for the Minneapolis Millers, on his way to a legendary career with the Giants.

an additional chore to do. So my mother was instrumental in making me a pull hitter. I learned that real quick."

Sometimes odd childhood variations on baseball might even have helped the future star develop unprecedented skills. In a remarkable interview with *The New York Times* in 1927, Paul Waner, a lifetime .333 hitter with Pittsburgh and other teams from the mid-1920s to the mid-1940s, revealed his secret:

There is nothing in the world that will take a freakish spin, a sudden hop, a wide, sweeping curve, like a corncob. The kids used to toss these cobs up as hard as they could. They would get hold of a short cob between the index finger and the thumb and let go. Whiz, it would come screaming up, and, believe me I mean it, they would scream. There were more curves in those corncob games than I have ever seen in a baseball game.

Well, I used to bat against those corncobs just as the other boys did, only I became obsessed with the idea of mastering the hitting of them. I really believe that this constant practice at hitting at those strange curves of the corncob did more than anything else to build up my batting. In the first place, it made my eyes keen. You had to keep your eyes peeled on the cob that came swishing up, because if it hit you in the eye it might blind you and if it hit you any place on the head it would hurt and probably leave a bad cut.

Many others also learned early on that ballplaying and pain can be inseparable companions. Hall of Fame catcher Ray Schalk, who starred with the Chicago White Sox from 1912 through the late 1920s, played his position even in childhood pick-up games: "I remember, after stopping several foul tips with my nose and other portions of my anatomy, I saved my pennies for many weeks until I was able to buy a catcher's mask," he said. "But even then I found I wasn't safe; one of the kids in making a wild lunge for the ball soaked me on the side of the head with his bat. There are times when a catcher needs a shield and helmet and a full suit of armor."

Sometimes a childhood injury changed the entire course of a player's career—perhaps even making the career possible. Probably the most famous example was Mordecai "Three-Finger" Brown, star pitcher with the Chicago Cubs early in the century, who as a child got his throwing hand caught in a corn chopper and had half of his index finger amputated and two other fingers damaged. This injury worked to Brown's advantage, as his unique grip gave him an almost unhittable variety of breaking pitches.

Less well remembered is the case of Tris Speaker, a brilliant hitter during his stints with Boston, Cleveland, and other teams from 1907 to 1928. "When but 10 years old I was thrown from a bronco and had my collarbone and right arm broken," he said in 1911, when he was already an established star with the Red Sox. "I was naturally a right-handed thrower, but was forced to use my left hand after the accident, and finally used my left hand for throwing altogether. I was a right-handed batter, but found my left arm was stronger, so I changed to batting from the left side."

Who knows what Speaker would have done from the right side, his "natural" side? As a lefty hitter, he compiled a lifetime batting average of .345, with a staggering 3,514 hits—the fifth-highest total ever in the major leagues.

Tris Speaker's golden left-handed stroke, with which he got 3,514 hits. Amazingly, the swing was the direct result of a near-crippling childhood injury.

To the Sandlot

Those with clearly prodigal skills soon graduated from pick-up games to more organized ball, in school or town leagues. But many future stars thought that this would be their last opportunity to play organized baseball; harboring no hopes of ever making it to the majors, most took (and thought they would always hold) "real" jobs, with baseball serving merely as an evening and weekend diversion.

Johnny Evers, the high-strung Hall of Fame second baseman for the Cubs, was one who had no illusions of a future in baseball, as he revealed in a 1914 interview describing his early days in Troy, New York:

I was never much of a ballplayer, and besides I was pretty light, so I was not particularly attacked with any fond hopes of becoming a great ball player. After finishing school—I attended the Christian Brothers' School—I learned the sign writer's trade—used to paint signs on windows and fences—you know what I mean. I was just setting on that for my life's trade, and was getting on nicely too, when I was taken sick with painters' colic, a disease contracted from the poisons in the paints.

Well, one day after that I happened to attend a ball game. It was on Labor Day, September 6, 1902. The Troy team was playing the Cuban Giants. So—I was a-settin' in the grandstand near the players' bench, watching them practice, when I heard the manager of the Troy team moaning the loss of his shortstop. It seemed that this player had been taken suddenly ill which left the team in a bad hole at the last moment. Well, sir, I heard them grumbling and swearing at the state of affairs until something happened to me—I could never describe it—I only know that I left my seat without a word to any one and vaulted over the rail to the players' bench, walked up to the manager, and told him that I was a ball player and to put me in the game as substitute for the sick shortstop.

That was instinct, I guess—I don't know what else. I had never even hoped to be a ballplayer before.

Well, the manager looked me over in a surprised sort of way—I felt myself getting smaller than I already was—and then said: "Get in a suit, kid; I guess you will have to do."

And Evers did, too, playing well enough that the sick player was never able to get his job back. Evers played regularly from that first game, hitting and fielding with the fire and skill that would distinguish his major-league career—a career that was to begin quite soon. "The Cubs got me from there the following season, 1903, and I have been with them pretty regular ever since," Evers said more than a decade later.

Still, not all future superstars have shown their skills on demand. Second baseman Eddie Collins, who hit .333 and collected 3,313 hits during a twenty-five-year career (1906–30) with the Athletics and White Sox, had a less pleasant experience on the sandlots of New York not long after Evers showed his stuff.

"I don't recall the name of the opposing nine in that first game," Collins told an interviewer in 1918, though he did recall that he pitched in the game. "The foe got something like a dozen hits off me and bunched a lot of them in the third inning. I recall vaguely now how I felt when we were so far behind, and

Opposite:
Paul Waner attributed some of his success as a hitter to swinging at hurled corncobs as a child.

it would not have taken much coaxing to have me abandon baseball forever."

Similarly shaky starts have characterized the early sandlot, high school, and college careers of many future Hall of Famers. Eddie Plank, who won 20 games seven times with the Philadelphia Athletics, recalled that he'd always seen baseball as little more than a "Fourth of July and Saturday amusement" before he started attending Gettysburg College as a twenty-five-year-old in 1900. "I was big and strong and fast and wild and inexperienced, and everything else that goes to make up a college pitcher," he said in 1910, midway through his career. "I simply shut my eyes and cut loose and most of those who didn't strike out got bases on balls, and I have suspected since that a lot of them struck out just to escape from standing up there at bat."

Mike Schmidt's experience in high school in Dayton, Ohio, made him doubt he'd ever succeed on a higher level, as he told *Pennsylvania Heritage* in 1995:

I was about the fourth or fifth best baseball player in school—a .250 hitter, and if you don't hit .400 in high school, nobody knows you're alive. . . . I tore up my left knee in football during my sophomore year and severely damaged my right knee the following year. Those two injuries curtailed all of the hopes I had to become a college athlete, let alone a major league baseball player. As it turned out, I went off to Ohio University with a T-square and a portfolio to study architecture, but I didn't give up on baseball. Since I didn't have an athletic scholarship, I was a "walk-on" who did eventually make the team. Looking back, I think it's ironic that had I not experienced those knee problems—which ended my football and basketball careers—I probably wouldn't have been a baseball player.

On the other hand, Johnny Mize's obvious slugging ability caught the eye of a nearby college coach while he was still in high school in the late 1920s. As Mize, a star with the Cardinals, Giants, and Yankees (1936–53), told the audience in his Hall of Fame induction speech in 1981:

I was fifteen years old, a sophomore in high school, and Harry Forrester, coach at Piedmont College, came up to me one day, I'd played a couple of baseball games, and he says, "Come out for the college team." I said, "You gotta be kidding." So he talked me into it. I think it was something like a Tuesday morning I went out, he said, "well, come out and at least put on a uniform." So I went out. Friday I was put in as a pinch-hitter, so I started out as a pinch-hitter and ended up as a pinch-hitter.

So I got a base hit, and the next day I started, and I finished the season. The next year . . . the boys wanted to know if I was going to play with them and I said, "I can't, I'm in high school." . . . So they said something to Mr. Forrester and he said, "Well, we'll fix it up. You can take one subject in college and you can play on the team." So I went out for the team and they didn't mention the subject and I didn't either.

Then we came around to next year and I just automatically went out and started playing when they started the first practice and probably made the only record that will never be broken—I don't know of any guy today that will play three years of college ball while still in high school.

"I was always the kid with potential," Mike Schmidt said—but that potential wasn't realized until his second full year in the majors.

Given the opportunity, of course, most players are thrilled at the chance to sign with a minor-league team, or even join a semipro circuit, both of which actually pay people to play baseball. But for many, a steady income has been only part of the equation. "Our aim in those days was not just to make money," said Eddie Collins, recalling his days with the Tarrytown (New York) Terrors and other semipro teams. "The fun we had overshadowed everything else."

Lucky it did, for semipro baseball did not pay well. "I played two summers up in Marvell, Arkansas, and worked in a drug store with my uncle," said Hall of Famer Travis Jackson, star shortstop for the New York Giants from 1922 to 1936. "They had an excellent bunch of semipro teams up in Marvell, Holly Grove, Clarendon, and Marianna, and so I jerked soda there in the daytime and at night and on Friday and Saturday we'd play ball games."

Getting a job with a professional team isn't always easy. When he graduated from Columbus (Georgia) High School in 1986, future White Sox superstar Frank Thomas expected that his glowing statistics would make him a prized commodity in the major-league draft. But they didn't, as Thomas told *Sport* magazine in 1994:

I was not drafted and I was shocked. There were about 20 guys in my area drafted, and none of those guys compared to what I accomplished. They had speed and other things I didn't have, but no one even came close to doing what I've done. Those guys didn't make it through A-ball. That's something I've never understood. The scouts told me I would never be a major-league player, and I told them, "A few years down the road, I'm going to cost you a little more than I would right now."

Thomas was right. Biding his time, he starred on Auburn University's baseball team; when he was finally drafted by the White Sox in 1989, he received a six-figure signing bonus—far more than would have been necessary to sign him out of high school. By a year later, he'd already proven himself to be a consistent .300 hitter with tremendous power and a phenomenal batting eye. Today Thomas is also, deservedly, one of the highest-paid players in baseball.

Take a glance at 5'8", 215-pound Kirby Puckett, and you'll probably see why scouts were cautious about his major-league potential. "I was told I would never make it because I was too short," he said just after his 1996 retirement. "Well, I'm still too short, but I've got ten All-Star Games, two World Series championships and I'm a very happy and contented guy."

In the face of negative reports, Thomas and Puckett maintained complete confidence that the scouts were wrong. On the other hand, no one ever doubted that slugging first baseman Orlando Cepeda had the talent to make the majors—except Cepeda himself, struggling through the transition from his native Puerto Rico to the United States of the late 1950s. "I don't think people understood how hard it was coming from a Latin country to play baseball in America," Cepeda told biographer Richard Keller in *Orlando Cepeda: The Baby Bull* (1987). "Everything was different. The language, the customs, the food. It was the first time I ever experienced racial prejudice. It didn't exist in Puerto Rico. It came as a shock to me."

As one of the first black ballplayers to follow Jackie Robinson into the majors, catcher Roy Campanella experienced a culture shock at least as rude as that felt by Cepeda. In Robinson's *Baseball Has Done It* (a 1964 book about the integration of baseball), Campanella told of the pressures of being in the vanguard of social change:

I broke into organized ball in New England, which was a part of the country where integration wasn't necessary—there weren't any Negroes in Nashua when Don Newcombe and I played there. We ran into difficulties in Lynn, Massachusetts. They had a manager down there who didn't particularly care to see Negroes in the league. He did his utmost to try to dishearten us. But when someone tries to dishearten you—I know I was like this and so was Newcombe—you'd try just that much harder. And when you try harder, it improves your ability.

Willie Stargell, who was raised in California, found his minor-league experience in Plainview, Texas, in 1959 even more disheartening, as he told the *New York Daily News* in 1988:

I had never seen segregation. Down there, it was the time of whites-only this, colored-only that. It was something ballclubs couldn't change, so I had to yield to it.

I got to the park early one day and was approached at the gate by two men. One was wearing a trenchcoat. It was a hot, muggy day, and I remember thinking it strange that someone would be wearing a coat.

"When I started playing baseball, it was like God said to me: 'I'm going to create certain situations to see how you deal with them,'" Willie Stargell said of the racial prejudice he had to face as a minor leaguer.

Then he opened the coat and took out a shotgun. He put it to my forehead and said, "Nigger, if you play today, I'll blow your brains out."

I couldn't talk to anyone about it. The two guys I roomed with, one was from Cuba and the other from the Dominican Republic, didn't speak English and I didn't speak Spanish.

I decided baseball was what I wanted to do, and I was going to play. There were fairgrounds next to the stadium, and a rodeo was going on. During the game, a car over there backfired. I fell to my knees and never felt so weak.

But, you know, I had a good game and never saw those guys again. That's when I was able to say that I wasn't going to let anybody or anything interfere with what I wanted to do.

The challenge before Lefty Grove, who eventually won 20 or more games seven years in a row with the Athletics on his way to 300 wins in the majors, was staying optimistic while traveling a long, circuitous route before finally reaching the bigs in 1925. Keeping his sense of self-worth was no easy task, as

Carl Hubbell delivers his out pitch,
the screwball, using a pitching motion
so odd and stressful that it almost
kept him out of the majors.

he discovered when he pitched for Martinsburg, West Virginia, in the Blue Ridge League. "I was up there for five weeks," he said. "Martinsburg had just built a fence around the ballpark, and they owed 'em $3500, so they sold me to Jack Dunn of the Orioles to get the $3500 to pay for the fence."

The problem longtime Giant ace Carl Hubbell faced was quite basic: convincing coaches and managers he could pitch. He had the most trouble proving that a new pitch he had developed—which would later make him famous—could effectively get batters out without ruining his arm.

Warming up with an old-time catcher when he joined a minor-league team in Oklahoma City in 1925, Hubbell unveiled his new pitch. The ball, released with a sharp twist of the arm and wrist toward the body, did not behave like a typical curve: It spun and broke in the opposite direction. The catcher, tossing the ball back, asked Hubbell to throw the same pitch again. "I threw it again and he said, 'Well, that's the screwiest damn pitch I ever saw,'" Hubbell recalled.

And so the screwball got its name.

Using his new pitch, Hubbell had a tremendous year at Oklahoma City, after which he was sold to the major-league Detroit Tigers. "You talk about somebody that was up in the clouds!" he said. But his visions of a future starring in major-league baseball weren't close to becoming a reality yet.

Ty Cobb was managing the Tigers in 1926, but it was a coach named George McBride who handled the rookies. "I started throwing the screwball and he said, 'What are you doing?' And I said, 'That's the screwball.' He replied, 'Christ sake, you're going to tear your arm up. Don't throw that.'"

So Hubbell didn't, not for the three years that the Tigers held onto him. At least partly as a result, he didn't look like much of a pitcher, and the Tigers never allowed him to pitch as much as a single inning in a spring-training game before sending him down to the minors. Finally, the Tigers gave up their rights to him, and Hubbell was dispatched to Beaumont in the Texas League, "the only club that wanted me, I guess, after three years," as he put it. "Hell, I should have had the word 'reject' written over my uniform."

But in Beaumont he was able at last to use the screwball again, and finally his luck began to turn. Dick Kinsella, a politician and part-time scout for John McGraw's Giants, was a delegate to the 1928 Democratic National Convention in Houston. One day, when nothing much was going on at the convention, Kinsella decided to go to a ball game—a game, as it happened, that pitted Houston against Beaumont, with Hubbell pitching.

As soon as the game was over—using his deadly breaking pitch, Hubbell had won, 2–1, in eleven innings—Kinsella hurried to the telephone and called McGraw with the exciting news that he had found a new potential star. "And by God, within about three or four days I was on my way to join the Giants," Hubbell said.

Kinsella and McGraw were the only individuals able to see beyond the "washout" tag that had attached itself to Hubbell during his three years in the Detroit system. Their instincts hadn't failed them, for King Carl went on to garner 253 victories in a sixteen-year career with the Giants, on his way to a 1947 election to the Hall of Fame. He didn't get to pitch his first major-league game until he was twenty-five years old, so it's likely that he would have been a 300-game winner if someone had recognized his outstanding ability earlier.

Making the Show

There's no bigger leap for a rising young star than the step from the minor leagues to the majors. Even Hall of Famers recall the rude shock they experienced on arriving at their first big-league training camp. Most had been superstars throughout their careers thus far, and had always been treated as such by their teammates. Now, suddenly, they were seen merely as potential usurpers of established major leaguers' jobs—in many ways, even more of an enemy than players on opposing teams.

This attitude was especially harsh in baseball's earlier days, when teams were fewer, salaries lower, and management didn't often see rookie stars as investments worth protecting. As second baseman Billy Herman, a star with the Cubs and other teams (1931–47), told Hall of Fame director Ken Smith in 1964, even if you were a hot prospect, "back quite a few years ago spring training was only to get your established stars in shape. The young boy didn't have much of a chance. He just had to go out and battle and fight and try to get what practice and attention he could."

Infielder Jimmy Dykes, an integral part of Philadelphia's three straight pennants (and two championships) in 1929–31 under the leadership of manager Connie Mack, shared with Ken Smith similar memories of his first call-up to the majors:

I reported to the Athletics fall, 1916. In those days, you didn't dress in the clubhouse with the ballplayers; they had a place where they kept the gas meters, and that's where they put the rookies. Mr. Mack finally took me by the hand and got me in the batter's box, because in those days you didn't go in that batter's box without permission. And I got up in there and you're only supposed to hit four, but I knew I wasn't gonna get back in there too soon and I hit about eight.

It took a larger-than-life personality—Babe Ruth's—to actually do what many a rookie must have wished he'd been able to: confront his teammates. Is it any surprise that Ruth took matters into his own hands when he found himself and two other rookie teammates being treated badly by Joe Wood, Tris Speaker, and the other established Red Sox stars in 1914? In a 1931 interview with columnist Frederick Lieb, the Babe explained his methods:

That Boston outfit was a pretty hard-boiled bunch to crash, and nobody seemed any too glad to see us. They put me in to pitch the very day we three reported to the club, and I won my game, 3 to 2. [Manager Bill] Carrigan told me I pitched a nice game, but that was the only praise I received.

The next day we were working out in front of the grandstand in preliminary fielding practice, tossing the ball back and forth to loosen up our arms. Joe Wood was playing toss with Speaker and failed to catch the ball. It rolled over to me. Being anxious to please, I retrieved the ball and tossed it to Joe. I thought he was expecting it, but apparently he wasn't looking and the ball hit him in the back. He was rather sore, and picking up the ball he threw it with all his might and hit me with it on the shin.

Before the game I asked Carrigan whether he would call a meeting of the players in the clubhouse before they went home.

Overleaf:
Babe Ruth (far left) with some Boston teammates, circa 1916. When the Babe arrived in Boston as a raw rookie two years earlier, his more established elders would never have let him (or any rookie) sit so close to them. "That Boston outfit was a pretty hard-boiled bunch to crash," Ruth recalled.

31

"What d'you want a meeting for, Babe?" he asked.

"Well, Bill, I've got something on my mind and I won't be any good until I get it off."

I told them I was a green kid of 20, just a few months out of a home, with little experience and knowledge of the world. I said I wanted to make good in baseball, wanted to mind my own business and sit back and learn something.

However, I added there were some people on the club who apparently didn't like me and resented my presence. So I suggested that we be permitted to fight it out. I said: "If they lick me, all right, and if I lick them, all right, but let it end there." And I suggested that my first opponents be Wood and Speaker.

No one took him up on the offer.

In his first spring training with the Yankees, Lou Gehrig dealt with potential confrontation with established big leaguers in a different way: by being as quiet and circumspect as possible. In 1923, after leaving Columbia University, he'd been signed by the Yankees and farmed out to Hartford. He even got into thirteen games with the Yanks (hitting .423 in 26 at bats), but the 1924 season was to be his first full year with the team. As he told columnist Frank Graham in 1931, Gehrig approached the season with great trepidation:

At last the day came to start for New Orleans, where the Yanks trained then. Money was scarce in our house and had been for some time, with my father sick and my mother and I trying to keep the house going.

Besides, my mother had been sick all through the summer and it had taken all the money we had put aside to pay the doctor's bills. When I picked up my bag and started for the train my mother gave me $12, which was really more than she could spare.

At New Orleans the races were on and our hotel was crowded so the management put a cot for me in the room assigned to [the older and more worldly] Benny Bengough and Hinkey Haines. Benny and Hinkey were nice to me, but after all, what could they say to me? . . . They were fellows who were used to having money and going around having good times and they'd sit there by the hour and talk to each other of their experiences while I'd sit on my cot and listen open mouthed.

Every night Hinkey and Benny and the other fellows would go somewhere—to dinner or to dance, or to the theater. I couldn't go any place. I couldn't even go to a picture show. But I didn't let on—didn't let anybody know that I was busy figuring all the time how I could pay my tips in the dining room and how glad I was we worked from 11 to 1 every day and I could skip lunch. So every night when the rest of them went out I went out too. But I went out to walk the streets for an hour or so, feeling lonesome and homesick and wishing I was back in New York.

The only one who suspected how things were with me was George Pipgras. George was a busher too, and he didn't have much more than I did, but he had a little more and I guess he felt sorry for me. He didn't say so, but one night he asked me if I'd like to have dinner with him at a nice restaurant in the French quarter. I accepted his invitation and off we went. When we got

there who did we see at a corner table but Joe Dugan and Whitey Witt. Lines were sharply drawn between the regulars and the rookies in those days and we were scared to sit down in the same restaurant with two famous players like Dugan and Witt. We almost ran out of the place and didn't slow down until we got back to the hotel. Then we were afraid they'd tell Hug [Manager Miller Huggins] we were stepping out and that he'd be sore on us and maybe release us. So we abandoned our plan altogether and stuck to the hotel.

Of course, rookies have always faced challenges other than those posed by their teammates. For many, the culture shock of a new city and the tumult of opening day was almost overwhelming—and was not allayed by unsympathetic managers who had more important things to think about. "I joined the White Sox August 11, 1912 . . . a youngster who had never seen a big-league ballgame," catcher Ray Schalk recalled. "Jim Callahan, the manager of the Chicago White Sox, gave me a ball and said, 'Boy, here's your pitcher, Doc White. God love your soul and may you rest in peace.'"

Some young players have been so awestruck at making the majors that they lost their self-confidence. "I'll never forget my first experience in a Philadelphia uniform," Eddie Collins told *The Sporting News*, recalling his rookie year of 1906:

Rube Waddell, one of the greatest lefthanders who ever threw a ball past a batter, had been warming up on the sidelines.

"Get a bat, kid," he said, "and I'll throw you a few."

With more fear than confidence, I took my stance at the plate. He threw me three curve balls that looked as though they'd dropped off a table. I missed all three. I guess if I had been standing up there yet I wouldn't have fouled one.

I was a pretty discouraged kid, as I walked away from the plate. But the Rube, probably noting my discouragement, walked up from the box and patted me on the back, saying, "Don't mind that, kid. I do that to 'em all."

Honus Wagner learned another rookie lesson the hard way. "I played half a season before I got up enough courage to speak to an opponent," he told *The Sporting News* in 1949. "I was in right field one day and after the other club's right fielder hit two successive home runs, I remarked as we exchanged positions, 'Nice hitting.' He gave me a dirty look and, in a sneering tone, said, 'Go to hell.'"

The greater the hype, the greater the pressure, as Mickey Mantle discovered when he joined the Yankees as a teenage rookie, manager Casey Stengel's new hot prospect. In an interview with Roy Firestone on ESPN, he described the experience:

In 1951 we went to spring training in Phoenix, and I must have hit 10 or 12 home runs, fifteen maybe; anyway, it was an unbelievable spring, and that's when they started writing that I was going to be the next Babe Ruth and Lou Gehrig and Joe DiMaggio all rolled up into one.

Well, it didn't happen. We go back to New York. I'm only nineteen years old, from Commerce, Oklahoma, and I think the biggest crowd I ever played for

Under Mom's watchful eye, Mickey Mantle looked every bit his age (nineteen) in 1951, at the dawn of his highly hyped rookie season with the Yankees. "In the locker room I never spoke to anyone," Mantle said of his painful early days as a major leaguer, "because I was simply too bashful to start a conversation."

Mickey Mantle, still just nineteen years old, in front of a gigantic crowd at Yankee Stadium. "What did begin to pierce my hide . . . was the virulence of some of the insults that were tossed at me from the nearby stands," Mantle said of fan reaction to his early-season struggles.

was like 500 people at Joplin, and I go to Yankee Stadium for the first time, and there's 68,000 people there and they're playing the Red Sox. Anyway, I started striking out quite a bit, and I lost my confidence. I struck out five straight times in a double-header up in Boston and Casey took me out of the game and put somebody else in.

Things didn't look up immediately for Mantle. Sent to the minors, he continued to struggle, at one time going 0 for 22 and almost quitting the game before regaining his confidence and his batting stroke.

But his stage fright upon arriving in the majors couldn't have been any more powerful than the stresses felt by twenty-two-year-old Larry Doby, the ballplayer who broke the color line in the American League. In *Baseball Has Done It*, he spoke of his call-up to the Cleveland Indians in 1947, which took place in Chicago as the Indians were about to play the White Sox:

The players were lined up in front of their lockers as if to meet a very important person. [Manager Lou] Boudreau introduced me to them, one by one. They shook my hand and said a few words, all except Lou Fleming, the first baseman. He turned his back. No one told me what I'd have to face. I was on my own. The Indians treated me like any other rookie. No one made friends with me. I had no roommate on trips. On trains no one invited me to play

Larry Doby's savior was Satchel Paige (left), who took the nervous younger man under his wing and reminded him that baseball was supposed to be fun. "What a roomie!" Doby said.

38

cards or talk over games. I couldn't stay with the club in the Del Prado Hotel in Chicago. I lived alone in a Negro hotel in St. Louis.

Loneliness made me tense up. Sitting on the bench day after day didn't help. No one seemed to know what I was supposed to do on the field, I was used only as a pinch hitter or runner. I struck out a lot because I tried too hard. Fans booed me in St. Louis, Washington, and Philadelphia. I worked out at second base and for the first time someone helped me, Joe Gordon, who gave me valuable tips about infield play. My average at the end of the season was .156. I thought I was through.

The Indians gave Doby another chance. But although he played better the next season, Doby's success in the majors was uncertain—until the Indians found someone who eased his loneliness: Satchel Paige, perhaps the most dominant pitcher in Negro League history. "I had a roomie at last—and what a roomie!" Doby said. "Satch arrived with twenty suits of clothes, a big smile, and no advice except to keep in there playing ball. Satch didn't care what people said or did. All he thought about was baseball."

Paige's arrival and Doby's own increasing self-confidence resulted in a 1948 season in which he hit .301. He followed that with eight consecutive seasons of 20 or more home runs and five seasons with more than 100 RBI.

Few have expressed the terror of the impending spotlight more clearly than Joe Sewell did in a 1982 interview with Walter Langford, as he described waiting to get into his first game with the Cleveland Indians in 1920:

I remember that I was sitting way down at one end of the bench watching. Doc Johnston was playing first base for Cleveland and he got five base hits in five times up and stole home. And Elmer Smith was playing right field and he went to right center and jumped as high as he could and caught a line drive like it was shot out of a cannon. Every time something would happen I'd crunch down deeper and deeper on the bench. I said to myself, "I ain't supposed to be up here." So the next day our manager Tris Speaker came out in the clubhouse before we were dressing and he came over to me and said, "Joe, you're playing shortstop today." I said to myself, "Oh, my God!" So there wasn't anything for me to do but get ready. . . .

We were playing the Athletics and old Scott Perry was pitching. I'll never forget old Scott. I ought to send him a Christmas card. Well, Tillie Walker was playing center field and the first time up I hit a ball to left center like a shot. Old Tillie just coasted over there and got it. The next time up—I'll never forget it—old Scott threw me a little old slider. . . . It came in on the outside of the plate and I hit that thing over the third baseman's head and away down there in the corner for three bases. Boy, I went around those bases just like I was flying—not even my toes seemed to touch the ground. When I got to third base I said to myself, "Shucks, this ain't so tough up here." And from that day till this I never have been nervous again.

Some future stars had no doubts, even at the start. Luis Aparicio, destined to become one of the finest shortstops in the American League during his years with the White Sox from the mid-1950s through the early 1960s, faced his

rookie season with the bravado he had developed on the ball fields in his native Venezuela. Shrugging off questions from reporters as to whether he was ready for the bigs, he said, "It is the same bat, the same ball, the same game as it is in Venezuela." He went on to hit .266 and lead the league in stolen bases during that 1956 season.

Ted Williams infuriated opposing teams with his brash self-confidence before he took his first regular-season swing for the Red Sox as a rookie in 1939. By the time the Sox opened the season against the Yankees, Williams had told everyone who'd listen how good he was. Even seeing Yankee stars Joe DiMaggio and Bill Dickey and Tommy Henrich and so many others up close, Williams made sure that he was not intimidated, as he recalled in *My Turn At Bat*:

I'm watching them, studying them all, and . . . I said to myself, I know I can hit as good as these guys. Just a young kid's reaction, seeing the greats, building up his confidence.

Red Ruffing was the Yankee pitcher. I watched him warm up, a big guy, I mean big, but a real easy-going style, like he didn't give a damn. When he came in with it, though, the ball whistled. I got up the first time and fouled one off, then he threw me a little curve and I fouled that one off too, then he struck me out on a high fastball. The second time up was the same thing: curve, curve, high fastball, strike three.

Well, here's this smart-talking kid rookie from California striking out his first two times up, and burning. I got to the bench and plopped down, and out of the corner of my eye I see ole Jack Wilson, one of our pitchers, coming to me. We'd been needling each other all spring, and I'd been telling him how I

was going to wear Ruffing out, and Jack's really got the old needle out now. He says, "Whata ya think of this league now, Bush?"

By this time I'm boiling. I said, "Screw you. That is one guy"—pointing at Ruffing—"I know I'm going to hit, and if he puts it in the same place again I'm riding it out of here."

Well it just so happened the next time up Ruffing got it high again, and I hit one to right center just a foot from going into the bleachers.

Williams never looked back. He finished the 1939 season with spectacular numbers: a .327 batting average, .609 slugging average, 44 doubles, 31 home runs, and a league-leading 145 RBI. And he hadn't turned twenty-one until August 30 of that year!

Undoubtedly the finest box score ever compiled by a future Hall of Famer playing his first major-league game belongs to Fred Clarke, the speedy outfielder with the Louisville Colonels and Pittsburgh Pirates from 1894 to 1915. Like many rookies, the slim Clarke looked like a child compared to the grizzled veterans as he entered the Louisville clubhouse for his first major league game. Compounding his troubles, he had brought an unusually small bat—atypically short and light by major-league standards—along with him from his last team, a minor-league club in Savannah, Georgia. In a 1946 letter to Ernest Lanigan, a historian at the Hall of Fame, Clarke recalled what happened next:

When I walked into the clubhouse with my little bat and was introduced one of the players asked me what I was going to do with the bat and informed me that the pitchers in the league would knock that out of my hand and I really believed them as I thought that players in the big league never made an error and made a hit every time they came to bat. . . . [I] went out and had that lucky day that made it possible for me to continue in the league. After the game I got my little bat and when I went into the clubhouse all the players was looking at me and I walked over and threw it in the bat box with the remark they had a hell of a time knocking it out of my hand today.

Clarke's lucky day? Five for five, including a triple—the first triple of 220 in a twenty-one-year major-league career that saw him hit .312 and steal 506 bases.

In another version of his story, Clarke returned to the clubhouse after his spectacular first game, tossed his bat at the feet of his teammates, and said, "You don't need a big bat to hit such bushers!" More likely, though, he was describing his real feelings in the 1946 letter: "If I had not had the good day I would not have been there long," he wrote, "for when I had a bad day the fans would think of the day I came in and give me another chance."

For Clarke and so many others, arrival in the big leagues was a stunning culmination of a lifelong dream. On some essential level, it was hard for most to believe that they really belonged, that they were, in fact, as talented as the stars they had admired from afar for so long.

Soon enough, the wonder and disbelief fade, though, and even future Hall of Famers learn what every player before them knew so well: Once you've made it to the majors, the hard work really begins.

Opposite:
Fred Clarke (left, with Pittsburgh teammates Tommy Leach and Honus Wagner), had the best first day in the major leagues of anyone in history.

Ty Cobb called Wheat's comment the best shor
But, like many baseball axioms, it doesn't prov
age to step to the plate and connect with a sm
can exceed ninety-five miles per hour. The fact
hitters have been unwilling or unable to analyz
fort of clichés. "I'm seeing the ball well," a slugg
are going badly, he may mutter, "The ball looks
it seems that the act of hitting a ball is as in
Listen to Jake Daubert, a star with Brooklyn a
century, when he was asked how he led the N
mark: "I honestly don't know. It's the hardest th
in the coal mines they used to do what they co
hold a heavy iron peg and the rest would swir
probably couldn't hit that peg at all. And yet, m
ing away with their full strength and never mi
at all. They do the right thing without thinkin
science and art of hitting. These players can al
challenges they face when they attempt to mai
grindingly long six-month season. Their joys
long history—knitting nineteenth-century stars
temporary hitters. Sometimes the science of bas

definition of batting ability he had ever heard.

e much insigh

white ball hu

over the history of baseball, many of the finest

their craft. Instead, they retreat behind the com-

will say when he's on a hot streak. When things

little as a pea to me these days." At such times,

plicable to the player as it is to the rest of us.

Cincinnati during the first two decades of this

tional League in hitting in 1913, with a .350

g in the world for me to explain. When I worked

ed 'pound the jumper.' That is, one man would

on it with sledge hammers. If you tried it you

who are used to such work can keep on pound-

though they hardly have their mind on the job

' Still, the occasional star is able to discuss the

be insightful and eloquent when describing the

ain a high quality of play over the course of a

nd frustrations form a tapestry over baseball's

ke Ed Delahanty to Tony Gwynn and other con-

all seems like a simple thing. "When you hit the

"I developed a contempt for pitchers."
—Zack Wheat, explaining how he hit .375 in 1924

The Batter's Eye

Ty Cobb called Wheat's comment the best short definition of batting ability he had ever heard. But, like many baseball axioms, it doesn't provide much insight into how the finest hitters manage to step to the plate and connect with a small white ball hurtling toward them at speeds that can exceed ninety-five miles per hour.

The fact is, over the history of baseball, many of the finest hitters have been unwilling or unable to analyze their craft. Instead, they retreat behind the comfort of clichés. "I'm seeing the ball well," a slugger will say when he's on a hot streak. When things are going badly, he may mutter, "The ball looks as little as a pea to me these days."

At such times, it seems that the act of hitting a ball is as inexplicable to the player as it is to the rest of us. Listen to Jake Daubert, a star with Brooklyn and Cincinnati during the first two decades of this century, when he was asked how he led the National League in hitting in 1913, with a .350 mark:

I honestly don't know. It's the hardest thing in the world for me to explain. When I worked in the coal mines they used to do what they called "pound the jumper." That is, one man would hold a heavy iron peg and the rest would swing on it with sledge hammers. If you tried it you probably couldn't hit that peg at all. And yet, men who are used to such work can keep on pounding away with their full strength and never miss, though they hardly have their mind on the job at all. They do the right thing without thinking.

Still, the occasional star is able to discuss the science and art of hitting. These players can also be insightful and eloquent when describing the challenges they face when they attempt to maintain a high quality of play over the course of a grindingly long six-month season. Their joys and frustrations form a tapestry over baseball's long history—knitting nineteenth-century stars like Ed Delahanty to Tony Gwynn and other contemporary hitters.

Sometimes the science of baseball seems like a simple thing. "When you hit the ball, and it carries for a home run, you can almost feel it in your arms as it leaves the home plate," said Jimmie Foxx, who surely knew what he was talking about—having had that feeling 534 times in his major-league career.

But the effortless swing that sends the ball rocketing into the distant stands is different for each player, as Hall of Fame slugger Hank Greenberg described in a *Collier's* article in 1939, the year after he hit 58 home runs for the Detroit Tigers:

Opposite:
"I felt like elbowing a pitcher out of the way when I met him," Zack Wheat said of his self-confidence as a hitter. "I could hit anything he had. I knew it and he knew it."

It's a funny thing about hitting home runs—you can't learn to do it from someone else. If I ever tried to bat as the Babe used to bat, I wouldn't hit three home runs a year. He batted with his back to the pitcher and he always swung, as he said, "in front of the ball." That is, he hit it before it reached the plate. If I ever tried to copy Joe DiMaggio's flat-footed stance or Joe Cronin's wide-open stance I'd wind up with even more strikeouts than I get now, and that's plenty.

Batting is a natural art. There are a few fundamentals you must learn but after that you're on your own. The only way you can learn to bat is to bat. I learned at high school many years ago. Since then I haven't learned an awful lot. I know that I still make the same mistakes I made then but there's nothing I can do about it. Those mistakes I make are so natural that I can't eradicate them.

Pitchers quickly identify such shortcomings and work to exploit them, no matter how good a hitter they face. How many times does a highly touted young slugger arrive in the majors and set the league on fire—but only on his first trip round the majors? (The answer is: It happens every season.)

By the time the rookie has accumulated a hundred or so at bats, the pitchers will have figured out the chinks in his armor—the big-breaking curve, maybe, or the fastball down and away. All over the league, pitchers will go to that pitch again and again, until the young slugger learns to adjust, or until he disappears once again into the minors.

It goes without saying that great hitters are the ones who can overcome their weaknesses. Hank Greenberg might modestly have claimed that he made the same mistakes throughout his career, and he surely meant what he said. But talk to any pitcher who had to face Greenberg (who hit 30 or more home runs six times in his career), and you'd hear the rest of the story. Sure, you could cross him up once in a while, get him to overstride and pull his head off the ball, but the next time you tried the same combination of pitches he'd be all over the ball. He had the ability to adjust.

So, of course, did Hank Aaron, along with a fierce inner drive that didn't permit him to be satisfied with his accomplishments, but always to want more. His determination came through clearly in an anecdote Aaron told in his 1968 autobiography, *Aaron, r.f.*. In it, Aaron remembered a conversation he'd had with sportswriter Bob Wolf early in his career with the Braves:

"Hank, I just heard you say that your first season was a disappointment to you," [Wolf] said. "You can't really be serious, can you?"

Then he pulled out the record. "Twenty-seven doubles, 13 home runs, 69 runs batted in and .280 average—I'd say that's pretty good for a rookie."

"Not if you been used to hitting .340 all your life," I said. "I was hitting over .400 with the Indianapolis Clowns."

"What do you think Willie Mays hit his first season in the big leagues? Or Ty Cobb, or Rogers Hornsby, or even your pal Ed Mathews? Neither one hit as much as you did. Cobb didn't hit but .240. Mays hit .274. And Hornsby, the great Hornsby, he didn't hit but .246."

"Still don't make me feel any better that I didn't hit but .280," I said.

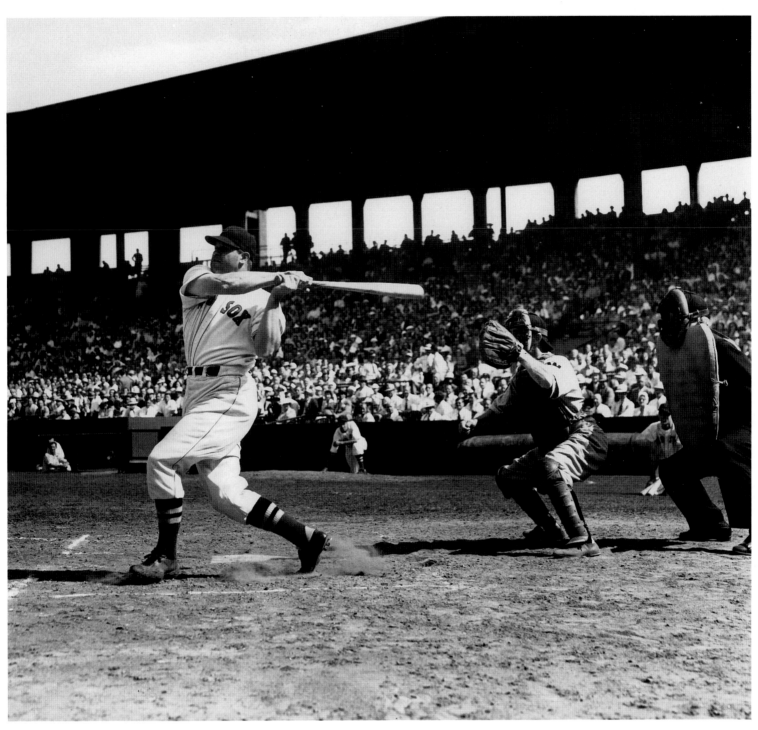

Jimmie Foxx, every inch a power hitter, smashing a home run—the 495th of his career—in 1940.

Even as a rookie in 1954, Hank Aaron knew he was destined for great things. Others weren't so sure, however. "To give you an idea of how important I was in 1954, on the Braves highlight film from that year, it showed me hitting a foul ball," Aaron said. "That was it."

"What did you expect to hit, .400?"

"Not my first season," I said. "Some day I'd like to hit .400. I guess that's really what I'd rather do than anything else in the big leagues, be the next player that hit .400. A lot of guys are hitting 40 home runs these days, and a lot of guys are driving in a lot of runs. But nobody has hit .400 since Ted Williams. I'd like to be the next one."

Hank Aaron never hit .400—his highest batting average was "just" .355. But he did leave his mark on the game in another way, surpassing Babe Ruth's career total of 714 home runs, a record long thought far less likely to be broken than the .400 barrier.

Aaron gave some insights into the effort required to become—and remain—a great hitter in a 1967 interview with the Hall of Fame's Ken Smith. "In order to be good at anything, you have to work at it," Aaron said. "I've always had a little ability, but I always work at my weakness and study opposing pitchers. . . . I know exactly what I can do at the plate, and I try to find out exactly what the opposing pitcher can do."

Adjusting to big-league pitching comes harder for some than others. In a 1974 interview published in *The New York Times*, Al Kaline discussed his struggles as a teenage prospect with the Tigers:

I was taught at a very young age—when I first joined the club, by the veterans that were there—that pitchers in the major leagues will pitch to your weakness. So I figured the first thing I had to do was find my weakness. When I first came up, they pitched me high and inside. I was thin, I wasn't very strong, and they figured they could take the bat right out of my hands. So during the winter of '54, before the '55 season, I tried to build myself up, work on my quickness, make my hands and arms strong.

The results of Kaline's hard work are written in the stats pages. In 1954, his first full season, he batted .276, with 18 doubles, 3 triples, 4 home runs, and 43

Opposite:

Hank Aaron's classic, predatory batting stance —one that culminated in a smooth swing that launched 755 home runs.

As a rookie in 1954, Al Kaline was overpowered by pitches up and in. His solution: Eliminate that weakness. The result: 3,000 career hits.

Opposite:

"I am not a little guy," said Babe Ruth—a fact that was not lost on fearful American League pitchers whenever the Babe swung his "pet war club."

52

RBI. One year later, in just eighty-eight more at bats, he improved those numbers to .340 (with 200 hits), 24 doubles, 8 triples, 27 home runs, and 102 RBI. His increased quickness and strength led to a Hall of Fame career with more than 3,000 hits and nine seasons with more than 20 home runs.

Not every hitter has to work so hard to develop strength. In a mid-career interview with *Baseball Magazine*'s F. C. Lane, the 6'2", 215-pound Babe Ruth acknowledged what even the most casual baseball fan already knows: He was a man of enormous—unique—physical stature:

I am not a little guy. Hitting hard is strength and weight as much as anything else. I am tall and heavy and strong in the arms and shoulders. And it isn't just strength and weight. Height and long arms are an advantage. A tall man, especially if his arms are long, can get a better swipe at a baseball than a shorter man of the same strength and weight.

Ruth lifted his huge hands, which were covered with calluses. "I got those from gripping this old war club," he told Lane. "The harder you grip the bat, the faster the ball will travel. When I am out after a homer, I try to make mush of this solid ash handle."

Not surprisingly, what worked for the Babe doesn't work for others. "You can't go up to the plate unless you're relaxed," future Hall of Famer Tony Gwynn said in 1991. "The tendency is to squeeze the bat. Squeeze the sawdust out of it. I wait and wait, and let the ball get right on top of me and just swing with a loose grip."

One of the things that make Gwynn such a phenomenal hitter is this ability to be patient, a virtue that is another hallmark of the best ballplayers. "As a hitter, I am always waiting for the hurler who has trouble getting the ball over the plate," Joe DiMaggio pointed out in 1939, early in his career. "Control and a pitcher's ability to obey the orders of the catcher combine to beat a hitter."

Patience is especially important for the leadoff hitter, whose primary job is to get on base. An intense, career-long focus on this goal has made Rickey Henderson the finest leadoff man in baseball history. "I've always thought the leadoff hitter sets the tone," he told *Sports Illustrated* in 1997. "If the starting pitcher comes out and gets the leadoff man on one pitch, it's bad. The leadoff hitter should work the count, make the pitcher know this isn't going to be easy. If the leadoff man looks at six or seven pitches, it gives everyone a chance to see what the pitcher has: velocity, break, what pitches are working and which aren't."

Rogers Hornsby's advice to a young hitter, given seventy years earlier, followed the same course. "The secret of good batting, in my opinion, is to hit only good balls," he said. "Let the bad ones alone. The pitcher must put the ball over the plate or pass you. You can afford to wait. Don't be led by impatience to go after bad balls. That's exactly what the pitcher is trying to make you do."

Of course, not every great hitter agreed with Hornsby's philosophy. "As far as my swinging at too many bad pitches is concerned, all I can say is that I like to swing at any ball that's close enough for me to reach and that I can see real good," Yogi Berra said in *Yogi* (1961). "If I had to give back all the hits I've got on balls that were outside the strike zone, I would be in tough shape."

Even when upright, Rickey Henderson, a classic leadoff man, presents an infuriatingly small strike zone to opposing pitchers.

Rogers Hornsby delivered a hitting lesson to aspiring ballplayers whenever he walked to the plate. "I am not the strongest man on the diamond by a good deal, but I don't need to be," he said. "I have strength where it is necessary to have it, and that is in my arms."

And who would have told him to do it any differently? Berra hit 358 home runs and drove in 1,430 runs in a nineteen-year career with the Yankees, helping lead them to an astounding fourteen World Series (during which he slugged 12 more homers). He also won three Most Valuable Player awards, one of only eight players to do so.

Another great player who won three MVP awards was Mike Schmidt. But Schmidt (who hit .196 his first full season in the majors before going on to slam 548 home runs in an eighteen-year Hall of Fame career) only gradually learned the batting approach that best suited him, as he told *Pennsylvania Heritage* in 1995:

Opposite:
"There isn't a guy in this league who can flat out throw the ball by you," said Tony Gwynn. "I can get a bat on anybody."

"One of the reasons for my consistency over the years was probably the flexible approach I took to hitting," Mike Schmidt explained. "I've always been a student of hitting, watching other players' styles, adopting different techniques if I think they will be more successful."

Opposite:
Hall of Famers and unlikely pals Willie Mays and manager Leo Durocher in 1954. Said Durocher, "After all the fathers I'd had watching over me in my own career, I had finally got me a son."

I stopped acting as though every trip to the plate was a life-or-death proposition. Instead of thinking I had to hit every pitch with every ounce of strength, I tried to pick out a good pitch and swing naturally. With the more relaxed attitude that came with experience, everything started to fall into place. I allowed my natural instincts to take over, to become more confident. And to be sure, a big part of my ability to succeed as a player was confidence, knowing that the people around me believed in my abilities as a professional athlete. Feeling comfortable with my surroundings enabled me to achieve that confidence and I really believe that it took me a year to create that kind of atmosphere for success.

Sometimes a recommendation made to a great hitter early in his career is especially simple and concrete. In his 1955 autobiography *Born to Play Ball*, Willie Mays tells of one of the best pieces of wisdom he ever received:

I can remember the third or fourth game I was with the Giants. I had come down the clubhouse steps at the Polo Grounds and was on my way in to the bench for the start of batting practice before a game when I heard a voice behind me.
    "Hey, Hubbell!"
    I turned around. It was [manager] Leo Durocher.
    I said, "What'd you call me?"
    "Hubbell," the Skip said.
    "Carl Hubbell?"
    "That's right."

"What for?"

"Because of the way you wear your pants," Durocher said. And it was true. I had the habit of wearing my baseball pants long and low, the legs going down well past the knees, the way Hubbell wore his.

Well, I laughed a little and started walking to the dugout. But again I heard Leo's voice behind me.

"Hey, Hubbell."

"What now?" I said.

"Pull the pants higher. Get the legs up."

"What for?" I said.

"Shorten your strike zone," Leo said.

And he was right, of course. The strike zone is between the shoulder and the knee. A guy who wears his pants so low you can't tell where the knees are may find an umpire calling a strike on a low pitch.

A certain amount of great hitting requires a specific type of luck: the luck to be perfectly suited to the idiosyncratic ballpark you happen to call your home. In the mid-1990s, for example, Andres Galarraga, Larry Walker, and other sluggers have been fortunate enough to play half their games in Coors Field for the Colorado Rockies. These men would be fine hitters anywhere, but their numbers are clearly inflated by playing eighty-one games in a hitter's park set a mile above sea level. Similarly, Roger Maris had true power, but he also took advantage of Yankee Stadium's short right-field porch during his magnificent 61–home run season.

On the other hand, while ballparks giveth, they also taketh away. Joe DiMaggio suffered from the "flaw" of hitting fly balls into Yankee Stadium's cavernous center and left fields. And conventional wisdom of the time had it that Ted Williams's power totals suffered by having Fenway Park as his home— because he was a left-handed dead-pull hitter and right field was by far the deepest part of Fenway.

Or did Williams suffer? In an interview with the Hall of Fame's Ken Smith in 1964, he explained that he saw it quite another way:

I enjoyed hitting at Fenway Park. I think that possibly it hurt my home run total a little bit, but I think that it possibly helped my batting average. . . .

Even though I had a long right-field fence I had a short left-field fence. Even though I didn't hit to left field too much, the big advantage I had regarding that was that I always felt that I could wait real good, because if I waited and even if I were a little late, it wasn't just a fly ball to the opposite field. I had a good chance of hitting it up against that short left-field fence.

The more patient the hitter, the longer he can wait before swinging, the greater bat control he has. Luke Appling, who struck out only 528 times in more than 10,000 plate appearances during a twenty-year career with the Chicago White Sox, once used his magnificent bat control to prove a point to the team's management.

Appling, a fan favorite, wanted to give away a dozen signed baseballs to area kids. But, as he told KMOX Radio in St. Louis in 1974, when he asked

Carl Yastrzemski's hitting stats, like Ted Williams's before him, were widely thought to have suffered due to Fenway Park's cavernous right field. But Yaz didn't agree, claiming that Fenway's green center-field background allowed him to see pitches clearly as they approached the plate. Opined Yaz: "In baseball, for the hitting part of it, a good background is a necessity—say, more so than a short ballpark or anything else."

the manager for the balls, he was sent upstairs to request them directly from club vice president Harry Grabiner.

I says, "I'd like to get a dozen balls, get 'em autographed," and he says, "Well, I tell you, we're running short of balls. If you want a dozen why don't you go down to the sporting goods and buy a dozen balls and get 'em autographed and then that'll solve your problem."

Billy Webb was coaching and I said, "You get a dozen balls and the first time the Yankees come into town on Sunday, one of them big games, Harry'll be down there and you get that batting practice pitcher to throw and I'll foul them twelve—I'll bet you a case of beer—I'll foul 'em into that damn stand." He said, "You wouldn't do it. I'll take you on."

So [the batting-practice pitcher] comes down there to start with, and he shines each ball up and threw 'em and I hit eleven of 'em into the stands and then Mr. Grabiner says, "Send him in. I'll give him a dozen balls."

Not every great hitter profits from patience. Big Ed Delahanty hit .346 during a sixteen-year career, but he always thought he was overeager at the plate. "If I could only hold myself like that old crab, Cap Anson [renowned for his patience and bat control], I would bat better than he ever did," Delahanty said. "But I can't. When the ball seems to me to be coming to my liking, I am going to belt it. I don't care where it comes, I'll either hit it or miss it, and if I miss it, God knows I'll miss it by enough."

At its heart, the extraordinary reflexes and skill needed to swing a bat and hit a ball coming at you eighty or ninety miles an hour may be innate and inexplicable. Maybe you've either got it or you don't.

Or maybe it's the bat. "My theory is the bigger the bat, the faster the ball will travel," Babe Ruth said to F. C. Lane in *Batting* (1925); Ruth's bludgeon weighed an astounding fifty-two ounces. "It's really the weight of the bat that drives the ball and I like a heavy bat. I have strength enough to swing it and when I meet the ball, I want to feel that I have something in my hands that will make it travel."

In Ruth's era, most sluggers seemed to compete to claim credit for the biggest possible bat. "My pet 'war club' weighs 48 ounces," Edd Roush told Lane. "I swing almost entirely with my arms, but the bat I use is so heavy and solid that when it meets the ball it will go for a hard drive anywhere."

But there were dissenters from the popular sentiment, even back then. "I weigh over 200 pounds," Hall of Famer Harry Heilman, who hit .342 in a career spent mostly with Detroit, told Lane, "and have height and strength enough to use a very heavy bat, if there were any sense in doing so. But I don't believe there is. Years ago I had an old club that weighed 40 ounces. My present bat weighs 36 ounces, but has plenty of wood. It is my belief that the weight of the bat has nothing to do with driving the ball hard."

When advice like this comes from a man who hit .403 one year (in 1923), and over .390 three other times, it seems like it might be worth listening to. And, in fact, not even the biggest slugger today swings a bat within ten ounces of Babe Ruth's old club. For fifty years now, lighter bats have been the norm—and one of the people most responsible for the change in style was Ted Williams.

"There's a lot of strength in those hands," Babe Ruth said of his enormous paws, which swung a bat that weighed a whopping 52 ounces.

In his 1971 book, *The Science of Hitting*, Williams discusses why he gave up his heavier bat:

I switched to a light bat as early as 1938, when I was with Minneapolis, the year before I went up with the Red Sox. It was in late August, and the weather was awful—hotter than I had ever seen it on the West Coast. I was having my first real good year in professional baseball, leading the American Association in batting, home runs, runs batted in, everything. But I was on base so much, swinging and running and sweating, that I felt wrung out.

One night we were in Columbus, another hot muggy night, and I happened to pick up one of Stan Spence's bats. What a light bat. A toothpick, the lightest in the rack. It was real pumpkin wood, too. You could see imprints all over it where the balls had hit. But it felt good in my hands. I'd been swinging a 35-ouncer, so I asked Stan if I could use it.

First time up, bases loaded, a little left-hander pitching, and the count went to 3 and 2. As I usually did in those cases, I choked up and said to myself, "I'm not going to strike out now, I'm going to get some wood on that ball," and he threw me a good pitch, low and away but just over the plate. I gave this bat a little flip, and I could hardly believe it—a home run to center field. Not the longest poke in the world, only 410 feet, but long enough.

That woke me up.

Stan Musial, in *Stan Musial: The Man's Own Story* (1964), was also in the vanguard of switching to lighter bats, shifting from thirty-three-ounce bats early in the season all the way to thirty-ounce ones late in the year. "The factories were surprised when I ordered bats weighing only 30 ounces. They doubted that they could get any good wood in bats so light," he recalled. "'Don't worry about the wood,' I said, 'make 'em up 30 ounces and send 'em.' If you hit a ball on the nose, it will go."

As did most other hitters in his time (the first decades of this century), Honus Wagner swung a heavy bat. But, as he told *Baseball Magazine* in 1918, no matter how fine the wood of the bats he used in the majors, he always pined for one he'd used all too briefly in an exhibition game years earlier:

There was never yet a perfect bat, and I don't suppose there ever can be. Not while the shape has to remain perfectly round and fouls can slip off the curving surface, and not while the material breaks just as you are administering a sure home run with the bases full. I have had bats break when I met the ball fair and square—break deliberately, after months of faithful service—and a feeble grounder would go trickling off the treacherous stick, when the force I put into the wallop had spelled at least three bases. Again, I've had bats break and the resulting tap would be so short that the infielders couldn't get it to first ahead of me, when it would have been a pop fly but for the breakage. Bats are strange and moody things, and sometimes I think Pete Browning was right when he used to talk to his bats and credit them with human understanding.

As I said, there never was a perfect bat but, some years ago, I handled one that was almost perfection. I had that bat for just a little while, and can never handle it again—it isn't in existence now. It was one day back in

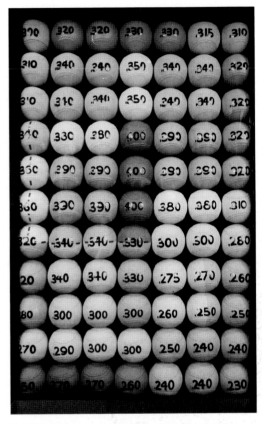

Ted Williams created this model of his hitting zones—with the number on each ball representing his likely batting average if every pitch crossed the plate at that location. The point: Even the Splendid Splinter could be pitched to, but the pitch had better not miss its spot by even an inch.

Opposite:
Luke Appling, "Old Aches and Pains," was a master of bat control during a twenty-year career with the White Sox.

Ted Williams's swing was a work of art with a lightweight bat.

Below:
In another vote for a light bat, late in the season, Stan Musial would use a 30-ouncer. No matter what weight bat you use, Musial said, "if you hit a ball on the nose, it will go."

The Ol' Perfesser's Baseball Brains

If there's one thing all great hitters have in common, it is absolute confidence that they can beat the pitcher at all games, mental and physical. During his playing career, Casey Stengel weighed in on managers who don't trust hitters' instincts. The following is from a 1918 issue of *Baseball Magazine*:

I am not one of the ball players with baseball brains. No, indeed. In fact, some people have told me that I was lacking in brains of any kind. The statement has been repeated so often that at times I have nursed a suspicion that perhaps it might be true. . . .

Why should a player have brains and initiative when so little is left to his judgment? If he can hit well to right field the manager tries to make him over into a machine that can grind out base hits to any field. If he is good at slugging the ball he is told to bunt. If he feels sure he can whale some particular pitcher a mile he has instructions to wait him out. . . . Very seldom are such things left to the discretion of the player.

Casey wrote these words when he was midway through a mediocre playing career. Three decades later, as manager of the New York Yankees, he became a legend, winning ten pennants in twelve years. And though he managed with iron precision—often platooning players who thought they should be in the lineup every day—he didn't forget his own frustrations at being overmanaged. Mickey Mantle, Yogi Berra, Hank Bauer, Moose Skowron, and many others blossomed under Stengel's reign. He trusted their baseball brains.

1898, when the Louisvilles were playing an exhibiti
small club in an Ohio river city. As luck would have it
being shipped to this little town, was sent on to the n
we found ourselves batless in the village. We figured, o
borrow bats from the locals, but we didn't need to.

Though he seemed ungainly at bat, Honus Wagner's talents were revealed by his career statistics: 3,418 hits and a lifetime batting average of .327. "He had no weakness," said fellow Hall of Famer Fred Clarke.

et. There was a spring and a texture to the wood that gave incomparable hit-ing power. Tap a fast ball with that bat, and it would go for two bases. Meet a curve, and you could send it to the bleachers. With that bat, a man who ordinarily hit .200 would be a .300 hitter, easy, and I blush to estimate the record I could have made with it.

All of us batted with that stick, rapping about twenty-eight long hits dur-ing the matinee. Between innings, I chatted with the kid who owned it, and he explained that he had laboriously turned the wood to proper shape him-self, and that it was originally the leg of an old fashioned, brokendown table that his grandfather possessed. It was some strange Oriental wood, some-what like mahogany, but much heavier and of firmer grain.

When the game ended, I turned to find the boy, intending to hand him good money for that bat, but the kid was gone. Apparently afraid we intended to steal his bat, he had caught it up and run like a whitehead. I never saw the boy again, and, although I twice played games in that town years after, he never came near the park. The mysterious bat, brimful of hits, vanished the same afternoon it first appeared, and its equal has never been discovered.

"I was endowed by nature with a restless ambition that would acknowledge no superior," said Ty Cobb (left, with perennial hitting rival Joe Jackson). "If I felt that another fellow had me beat, I was never easy in my own mind until I had surpassed him."

The Batting Evil Eye

Ty Cobb left an enormous footprint on major-league baseball during the first three decades of this century—not least in his belief that psychology was a powerful tool that could mean the difference between victory and defeat. Cobb gave an example of this in *Batting* (1925), showing how he defended his 1915 N.L. batting title both on and off the field:

The champion always has a decided advantage, be it baseball, boxing, or anything else. The contender lacks something of the champion's confidence and that is what beats him. I remember, I think it was in 1916, that Joe Jackson started out at a tremendous pace. He was going to get me that year sure. He came into the clubhouse and told me he was going to get me. I laughed at him, whereupon he grew earnest and offered to bet. "All right, Joe," said I. "I will bet you five hundred dollars that I beat you out this season." He thought it over for a minute but he didn't bet. That game I believe I made two or three hits and he made but one. Next day I walked over to the bench where he was sitting. He spoke to me, but I did not answer him. I knew he would be puzzled. A little later I walked over again. I thought he might have imagined I didn't hear him speak, so I looked at him, straight in the eye, until I got very close. He spoke to me again, but I made no reply. I knew what was in his mind. He was wondering, "What's he sore about now." And he didn't make any hits at all that game. The final game, I walked over with a broad smile, clapped him on the back and said, in the most friendly way, "Joe, Old Boy, how are you?" This seemed to astonish him more than anything else. All the rest of the season I had his goat, and I beat him out by forty points.

A check of the records shows that, in fact, Ty Cobb hit .371 in 1916, while Jackson batted "only" .341. Poor Joe.

But what Cobb neglected to mention was that Indian center fielder Tris Speaker posted a .386 mark that year to win the batting championship. It seems that Speaker was immune to Cobb's psychological trickery—or perhaps Cobb was spending so much time worrying about out-psyching Jackson that he failed to notice what was going on in Cleveland.

Baseball history is filled with talented, speedy ballplayers with no idea of how to run the bases. They can match Olympic sprinters stride for stride in a straight race, but put them on first after a single and they are just as likely to be tagged out at second as to steal the base.

Players who run the bases fundamentally well rely on extensive practice and an instinctive sense of the game situation and what it demands from them on the basepaths. When asked what was necessary to make a player into a first-class baserunner, speedy shortstop Bill Dahlen, renowned for his baserunning during a two-decade career at the turn of the century, summed it up: "Speed, of course; ability to get away quick; a good nerve, and a quick brain."

And speed isn't of the utmost importance, Dahlen went on. "Lots of fair baserunners achieve their results through sheer headwork. These you will see helpless almost, when it comes to getting down to first on an infield hit, for here there is no chance to 'beat the gate' on anybody. But once on the bags, there are several players whose good headwork invariably gets them along the bases."

Those who run the bases brilliantly—those who change the game the moment they get to first—seem possessed of more than "good headwork." They have an almost unearthly ability always to know what the pitcher is going to throw next, where the ball is going when it's hit, and who will be fielding it.

The most famous and controversial name in the pantheon of brilliant baserunners is certainly Ty Cobb. For Cobb, the art of baserunning began by keeping his legs in peak condition—and not only during the season, as he said in a 1930 interview:

I built up my legs in two ways: I hunted all through the winter, frequently walking all day long. I almost lived on my legs. In addition, I always hunted in heavy boots. When the training season opened, I fixed a piece of lead to my shoes. I took the lead off when the pennant race opened, and I felt as if I could run faster. . . . If you want good legs, you have to put them to work. I never gave mine any holidays.

Cobb loved to talk about baserunning, how even something as simple as taking an extra base can psych out the opponent and mean the difference between a victory and defeat. The following example is from a 1917 issue of *Baseball Magazine.*

Not even a home run with the bases crammed can quite demoralize an infield and get the defense up in the air as clever base running can do.

Such base running strikes deep at the foundation of the defense. It destroys confidence and when confidence is gone everything is gone. When a fast runner gets to first base and then starts running wild and gets away with it, he completely demoralizes the infield and gets the pitcher and catcher up in the air as well. Infielders get to throwing the ball around, missing plays, making errors and looking like a lot of boobs. They become completely rattled and when a ballplayer is rattled he is done for the time being. He might just as well take off his uniform and go to the club house.

In his interview, Cobb enlarged on this theory. "I believed in putting up a mental hazard for the other fellow," he said. "If we were five or six runs ahead,

Even in the off-season, the great Ty Cobb stayed in fighting trim, keeping his legs strong by hunting in heavy boots. "I almost lived on my legs," he recalled.

Cool Papa Bell, perhaps the most brilliant baserunner in the Negro Leagues. "Whatever you heard about him was the truth," said fellow Hall of Famer Judy Johnson. "He was the fastest man who ever put on a pair of baseball shoes.

I'd try some wild play, such as going from first to home on a single. This helped to make the other side hurry the play in a close game later on. I worked out all the angles I could think of to keep them guessing and hurrying. Every play was a problem of some sort."

Hall of Famer Cool Papa Bell, a Negro League star, used similar methods to get inside opponents' heads, as he revealed in a 1979 interview:

I could point down—if I'm on second base, I could point that way to [the batter], tell him to bunt it. He'll bunt it to third base, when he bunts it to third base, the third baseman comes to get the ball, and I score on it from second base. . . . The same way if I'm on first base, and I tell him to bunt the ball to third base, I go all the way to third. When they bunted the ball when I was on base, if I didn't go no further than second, they didn't think I did anything. . . .

But they caught me in different times. When you play against a team a lot of times, they'd catch your tricks, you know. He would bunt that ball, I'd be running, and I'd turn second base, and instead of them throwing to first base, they'd catch me between third and second base. They'd know I was going to third, so they'd catch me there. . . . But when we played a team that never played against us, oh, I could just do anything.

Fred Clarke claiming home plate early in this century. "You don't see the players sharpening their spikes to a fine point as we did," Clarke said in criticism of the modern game in 1960. "I can still see the game in which the Giants were out in front of their dugout sharpening spikes. I sent one of our boys after newspapers and we proceeded to cut strips of paper on our spikes—just to show [Giants manager John] McGraw and his gang ours also were plenty sharp."

More than any other aspect of the game except pitching, the best base-running involves a great degree of intimidation. "Kept my spikes sharp, I did," said Hall of Fame outfielder Edd Roush, and he wasn't the only one. "Hey Krauthead, I'm coming down on the next pitch!" is what baserunner Ty Cobb said to shortstop Honus Wagner in the 1909 World Series. When Cobb kept his promise, Wagner just happened to tag him on his face, opening up a gash on Cobb's lip that required a couple of stitches to repair.

In his very first game with the Montreal Royals (a Brooklyn Dodgers' minor-league team) in 1946, Jackie Robinson showed how baserunning aggressiveness can dominate a game. Early in the game, played against the Jersey City team, Robinson quelled any butterflies he might have been feeling by belting a three-run homer. When he came to bat in the fifth inning, he decided to try something different, as he recounted in 1960's *Wait Till Next Year*:

Instead of trying to slam the ball over the fence, I dropped a bunt down the third base line that caught the third baseman flatfooted. By the time he reached the slowly dribbling ball I had crossed first base. I remembered [Dodger general manager Branch] Rickey's advice to run those bases like crazy, so as the pitcher took his stretch I dashed daringly off first, then

Ty Cobb, the most feared baserunner of his time. Aggressive play on the bases, he said, "strikes deep at the foundation of the defense. It destroys confidence, and when confidence is gone everything is gone."

A classic Jackie Robinson slide, and another run stolen. "Above anything else," Robinson said, "I hate to lose."

plunged back on my belly as the catcher faked a throw to first. When the pitcher began his stretch for the second pitch I dashed off recklessly again, but I kept going this time and stole second easily.

I dashed off second now, still trying to worry Larry Higgins, the New Jersey pitcher. He broke off an inside curve which Tom Tatum slapped hard on the ground to the third baseman. A standard rule in baseball is that a man on second does not try to advance when the ball is hit to third base or shortstop. I acted as if I were going back to second, but when third baseman Norm Jaeger threw to first I dashed toward third. The first baseman fired right back to Jaeger, but I slid into third, beating the throw by an eyelash. I had now stolen one base officially, and had "taken" third, although it never would appear in the record as a stolen base. I figured now was the time to be daring. I would try to steal home!

Phil Otis came in to pitch for Jersey City. After his warm-up throws, I began to dance down the base line. He looked toward home plate, then threw hard to third, but I slid back in safely. I danced down the line and he threw to third again, but I slid back safely. I knew now that Otis was worried. He watched me closely and then fired to the plate as I ran halfway down the base line, dashing back to third before the catcher could throw me out. On the next pitch I again dashed down the base line. Otis was so frustrated that he stopped his delivery toward home plate—a balk. The umpire waved me on to the plate and a score.

Similar scenes—ones that often culminated in Robinson's stealing home—became a familiar sight to baseball fans as soon as Robinson joined the Dodgers in 1947. People who saw him play said he did more on the basepaths to change the course of a game than any other player of his time.

"Being fast is only the beginning," said Lou Brock, base stealer extraordinaire. "You have to learn the habit of every pitcher you'll face, just as the hitters do."

For Hall of Famer Max Carey, perfect balance was one secret of successful base stealing.

The aggressiveness that Robinson showed—essential in the best base-runners—must be wedded to a scientific study of pitchers if a fast runner is to become a fine base stealer. "Basically, good base runners all have to have the same things," said Lou Brock, who stole 938 bases—the second most ever—during a long career spent mostly with the Cardinals. "You have to have speed and quick reflexes. After that you succeed or fail on what you can learn by observation."

Max Carey, who stole 738 bases in a Hall of Fame career with the Pirates and other teams, let readers in on his secrets in a 1920 book entitled *How to Play the Outfield and How to Steal Bases.* Perhaps most important of all, Carey wrote, was the need to get a good jump while the pitcher was delivering the ball:

A good start or jump depends on two things:

1. Perfect balance, *which enables the runner to go either way, back to first or on to second, without loss of time. This balance is probably the most important part of a successful base stealer's stock in trade and the size of his lead depends on the command he has of his balance.*

2. Study of the pitcher's motion of delivery, *which means that the brain instantly puts the muscles of the legs and body into action at the slightest suggestion from the pitcher's motion as to where he will throw the ball. A runner jumping up and down naturally cannot study a pitcher's motion as well as one who is perfectly still.*

This department of base stealing is the hardest to master and is probably the secret of why some players never learn to steal bases—lack of co-ordination between brain and muscle. The reaction in some fast men may be a great deal slower than in some who are slower of foot yet get there just as fast because of an alert brain which puts them under way much sooner.

In his 1930 radio interview, Ty Cobb, who included 892 stolen bases in his eye-popping lifetime offensive totals, agreed with Carey's theories, and then added some fascinating inside information. "The two most important things in base stealing are getting the jump on the pitcher and making your slide away from the baseman," Cobb explained. "In stealing bases, I always watched the baseman's eyes, to know where the ball was coming. His eyes had to watch the ball. I didn't have the time for this, but his eyes told me. And then I knew where to throw my body away from the baseman."

This intelligence—the sense Cobb gave throughout his career that his mind was working faster and on more levels than anyone else's on the field—seems to have been shared by every great base stealer in baseball history. What is also

The cobra-like stare of Rickey Henderson, the greatest base stealer in the game's history.

shared was a sense of supreme confidence, a belief that the runner was simply superior to the pitcher and catcher who would try to catch him stealing.

Rickey Henderson, whose robust self-image drove opponents mad from the moment he first appeared in the majors in 1979, put it well. "You shouldn't have any fear as a base stealer," he said in a 1991 article in *Sport.* "Fear causes a lot of great runners not to steal. I've never had fear. If you throw me out, it makes me want to get up and beat you more."

In a 1975 *New York Times* article, Hall of Famer Joe Morgan—two-time Most Valuable Player with the Cincinnati Reds and known as the best baserunner of his era—said the same thing in a different way. "You have to work harder at stealing than anything else," he said. "I work harder at stealing than pitchers work at holding me on so I should be better than they are."

In the same article, Morgan also showed how a stolen-base threat can be such a disruptive force in a game:

When you're a base stealer, you cause things to happen. The pitcher worries about you, the catcher knows you're there and the fielders know you're there. You can do a lot of things to the defense. A lot of times I get on first base during the season and have no idea of stealing. But if I give them the impression I'm going to maybe they'll give [Johnny] Bench better pitches. If you're just going to stand over at first base, you're not going to help anybody.

But it was Lou Brock who probably best captured the spirit that possesses all great base thieves. "You're alone in a sea of enemies," he told *The New York Times* in 1982. "The only way you can hold your own is by arrogance, the ability to stand before the crowd. Every time you get thrown out, you've got to believe that somebody owes you four or five steals. Then you've got to go out and get them."

Joe Morgan, evading a tag from Boston first baseman Carl Yastrzemski in Game Five of the 1975 World Series. "The thing is," Morgan said, "a good runner can do something to win a game every single day."

Opposite:
Lou Brock, hoisting stolen base number 893— the one that broke Ty Cobb's career record.

Cap Anson also described the slow adoption of
duction: "Undoubtedly, many a player with s
taken a common driving glove, cut off the finge
the sting, but the first glove for baseball work ex
was made of buckskin, with sole leather tips on
in a hurry, and then the first basemen began to
scorned to protect the hands. They stopped the
and dragged in the bullet-throws, bare-pawed,
couldn't get a professional fielder to play toss-
shudder with terror at the thought of facing the
of making a springbox of the fingers, the ball se
down even the hottest liners that way, though
of the infielders and the catchers were awful s
when bleeding fingers were useless at the broker
gloves were in general use, they tended to be t
hand than to help him catch the ball. Old-timer
as halcyon days—a time when men were mer
enormous number of errors. One example: Rab
played for twenty-three years (1912–35). He u
those years, he led the league exactly one time i
ended his career with a .258 batting average.

e glove by proud major leaguers after its intro-

e or tender hands had ofte e,

and padded the palm with se

sively was turned out some 35 years back, and

e fingers. The catchers took up this style of glove

e them. But the rest of the stars, even to a team,

urderous liners, scooped the tearing grounders,

d with fingers gnarled and twisted. Today, you

ch without his precious glove, and they would

atsmen with the old bare hands. We had a trick

m hitting against the palm, and we could haul

ken fingers happened now and then. The hands

ts, as a rule, but they stuck to their work even

ints." Even by early this century, when fielder's

and stiff, and did more to protect the fielder's

players and fans alike) tend to remember those

but the fact is, even the best fielders made an

Maranville was a Hall of Fame shortstop who

n't much of an offensive threat—in fact, in all

ne offensive category (at bats in 1922), and he

t got Maranville into the Hall was his fielding,

While the ability to hit a major-league fastball is beyond most of our imagining, almost everyone who has played baseball or softball has had the pleasure of making a spectacular fielding play, at least once in a while: the running catch of a deep fly ball, the diving stab of a line drive, the clean pick of a ground ball and a hard toss of the ball into the first baseman's glove to nip the runner by a stride.

Robbing a great slugger of a hit is, well, at least something that *could* happen. But to be able to do it consistently, to snare grounders at third base as Brooks Robinson did, or unleash laser throws from the outfield à la Roberto Clemente—that takes extraordinary skill, terrific baseball smarts, and hard, hard work. It may have looked easy, but playing the field well day in and day out was difficult even for Ozzie Smith.

Of course, it used to be even more difficult, in the olden days of small, inflexible gloves—or even no gloves at all. Until the late nineteenth century, the fielders in professional baseball games played bare-handed. And even after a few individuals began to use gloves, many others scorned the practice.

In *America's National Game* (1911), former player, sportswriter, and sporting-goods entrepreneur Albert Spalding said that the first glove he ever saw on the hand of a ballplayer in a game was worn by one Charles Waite, a first baseman from New Haven, in 1875. "I asked Waite about his glove," Spalding wrote. "He confessed that he was a bit ashamed to wear it, but had it on to save his hand. He also admitted that he had chosen a color as inconspicuous as possible, because he didn't care to attract attention."

In a 1918 *Baseball Magazine* interview, Cap Anson also described the slow adoption of the glove by proud major leaguers after its introduction:

Undoubtedly, many a player with sore or tender hands had often, before this time, taken a common driving glove, cut off the fingers, and padded the palm with grass or felt to ease the sting, but the first glove for baseball work exclusively was turned out some 35 years back, and was made of buckskin, with sole leather tips on the fingers. The catchers took up this style of glove in a hurry, and then the first basemen began to use them. But the rest of the stars, even to a team, scorned to protect the hands. They stopped the murderous liners, scooped the tearing grounders, and dragged in the bullet-throws, barepawed, and with fingers gnarled and twisted. Today, you couldn't get a professional fielder to play toss-catch without his precious glove, and they would shudder with terror at the thought of facing the batsmen with the old bare hands.

We had a trick of making a springbox of the fingers, the ball seldom hitting against the palm, and we could haul down even the hottest liners that way,

Cap Anson demonstrating a typical baseball scene of the olden days. With slippery, dirty balls, bumpy fields, and small, tattered gloves, is it any wonder that teams regularly committed 300, even 400 errors a season, compared to only about 100 per season today?

Opposite:
Cap Anson, in the days before the glove. "We had a trick of making a springbox of the fingers," Anson said, "and we could haul down even the hottest liners that way, though broken fingers happened now and then."

81

Rabbit Maranville, who overcame the difficult—and even dangerous—conditions of his time to ride his fielding ability into the Hall of Fame. Commenting on the serious injuries he suffered playing baseball early in this century, Maranville said, "It wasn't the prospect of pain that scared me; it was the prospect of idleness."

though broken fingers happened now and then. The hands of the infielders and the catchers were awful sights, as a rule, but they stuck to their work even when bleeding fingers were useless at the broken joints.

Even by early this century, when fielder's gloves were in general use, they tended to be tiny and stiff, and did more to protect the fielder's hand than to help him catch the ball. Old-timers (players and fans alike) tend to remember those as halcyon days—a time when men were men—but the fact is, even the best fielders made an enormous number of errors.

One example: Rabbit Maranville was a Hall of Fame shortstop who played for twenty-three years (1912–35). He wasn't much of an offensive threat—in fact, in all those years, he led the league exactly one time in one offensive category (at bats in 1922), and he ended his career with a .258 batting average.

What got Maranville into the Hall was his fielding, along with such intangibles as "leadership." And by all accounts, Maranville *was* a brilliant fielder, possessing great range, sure hands, and a strong arm. But Maranville regularly committed 30, 40, even 50 errors in a season, and in 1914 he made 65 errors, a total that would send a player today on a one-way trip to the minors. Still, Maranville played in the majors for two more decades after that season.

Contrast Maranville's numbers—or those of Honus Wagner, a superb fielder who committed 40 or more errors in twelve different seasons—with those of Ozzie Smith, the most brilliant shortstop of this era. In 1978, his rookie year with the San Diego Padres, Smith made 25 errors. His fielding percentage was .970, one that Rabbit Maranville and other early infielders rarely approached.

Yet Ozzie Smith was roasted in the press for not living up to his clippings as a fielder. During a career spanning nearly twenty years, he never made as many as 25 errors again.

Infielders were not the only ones who fumbled often in earlier eras. Tris Speaker, dubbed "the greatest outfielder who ever lived" by journalists during

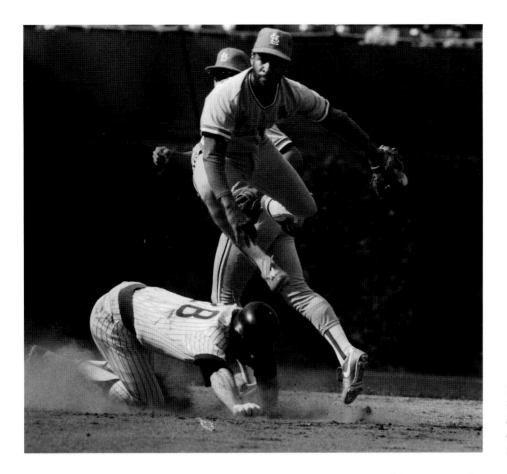

Ozzie Smith, with the big, flexible glove now in use. "I think it's a matter of never feeling limited, never limiting yourself in believing and feeling that you can do whatever you want to," said Smith of his fielding brilliance.

his twenty-two–year career (1907–28), committed as many as 25 errors in the outfield in a single season. By the time Willie Mays and Mickey Mantle were patrolling the outfield in the 1950s, an outfielder might make six or eight errors a year, but no more.

The point isn't that today's fielders are "good" while yesterday's were "bad." Before the design of capacious modern gloves, ballplayers did the best with what they had—whether it was bare hands or inadequate gloves.

And there were other reasons for those lower fielding percentages. Before a series of rules changes in the late 1910s and early 1920s, balls in use were always discolored by mud, spit, tobacco juice, petroleum jelly, and other substances—and were rarely replaced unless they were hit out of play. So in those days an infielder, for example, had to see and catch a dark ball against a dark background, and then grasp and throw the wet, slippery object to a fielder wearing an almost useless glove.

Not to mention the fact that they played on rough, chopped-up fields. Or the fact that stadiums didn't have lights, so games would frequently be played in fog, twilight, or other adverse conditions.

So there's an argument to be made as to which generation had the best fielders—though it's clear that today's games are far cleaner and more error-free than those of baseball's "Golden Age." And there's also no argument that, since baseball began, the best fielders have demonstrated not only spectacular reflexes, strength, and accuracy, but also some of the keenest minds ever seen in any professional sport.

Catcher

The most thoughtful and intelligent of all the fielders is also the only one who plays in foul territory: the catcher. Or at least that's what catchers have always said. And they're likely to add that they've got the hardest job on the diamond—figuring out what the pitcher should throw, catching the ball once it's thrown, gunning down baserunners, and dealing with the bumps and bruises that are their everyday lot.

In a 1939 *Sporting News* interview, the Yankees' catcher Bill Dickey, then in the midst of a seventeen-year career that would lead to the Hall of Fame, listed his prerequisites for succeeding at this challenging position:

(1)—A catcher must want to catch. He must make up his mind that it isn't the terrible job it is painted, and that he isn't going to say almost every day, "Why, oh why, with so many other positions in baseball, did I take up this hard job?"

(2)—A backstop must learn not to get discouraged, and must be ready to take it. Getting banged up, being knocked over are all in a day's work.

(3)—He must devote all his spare time at the park to mastering the trick of catching low balls. Anybody can catch a high ball. But to take low pitching right, that's the real trade-mark.

(4)—He has to impress it on himself that throwing is the softest part of his work and must come automatically. He must get the ball away, fast, smoothly. I never found that difficult.

(5)—The catcher must make the pitcher glad he has that particular backstop working with him. He must build up the pitcher's confidence, and that means studying the hitters.

Having duly noted "Dickey's Rules," the interviewer asked Dickey to talk about the fun of catching. Dickey laughed. "If you mean funny stories—well, from where we catchers operate there isn't much frolic," he said. "It's all serious business and you don't dare take your mind or your eyes off the job at hand."

All this responsibility requires the catcher to be able to think—and think quickly. An early spectacular example of the catcher's art was relayed by John McGraw (himself a Hall of Fame third baseman and manager), recalling a play made by Mike "King" Kelly, who revolutionized the position in the 1870s and 1880s:

The greatest play, from the standpoint of quick thinking, that I have ever seen, was one made by Mike Kelly years ago. It illustrates why they called Mike the King.

Kelly was catching in a close game. In the ninth inning his team led by a run, when the other side stepped to bat. Two men were retired easily. Then a base on balls and an error put the tying run on second and the winning run on first.

The next batter shot a hot single to right, and the man on second tore for the plate. The outfielder's throw came in true enough, but to Kelly's left, on his gloved hand. As the ball was in the air Mike saw that he had to take it with his left hand. If he used two hands he would miss the runner. Yet taking the

"From where we catchers operate there isn't much frolic," said Yankee Hall of Famer Bill Dickey. "It's all serious business and you don't dare take your mind or your eyes off the job at hand."

ball with the glove and swinging into a sliding man, he ran the chance of dropping the throw.

Kelly figured this out quicker than it takes me to tell it. He flung off his glove, caught the bounding ball with his bared left hand and touched the runner out.

I've seen many great plays in my twenty-seven years in baseball. This one has always stood out as the headiest play of them all.

In a 1920 interview with *Baseball Magazine*, Hall of Famer Ray Schalk thought the catcher deserved more credit than he received for preventing a great slugger—such as Babe Ruth—from getting hold of a pitch and sending it out of the park:

Babe Ruth is the toughest problem which confronts the American League catcher today. Notice, I don't say American League pitcher. I realize that the pitcher has his troubles when he sees Babe lumbering up to the plate, swinging those two big bats of his. But the chief burden of foiling Babe's murderous intentions on the baseball rests squarely upon the other partner of the battery. For in the last analysis, it is the catcher rather than the pitcher whose task it is to outguess the batter.

I know that many reams of paper have been covered with vivid descriptions of the duel which is always taking place between the man who toes the slab and the man who swings the ash. The public can understand that duel, for they can see what the pitcher as well as the batter is doing and can readily follow the success which favors first one and then the other of these hereditary enemies. But the far deeper, and I believe more important duel which is forever going on between the batter and the catcher, is hidden from the eyes of the spectator and most, if not all, of the intricate moves in that duel escape his notice. For this reason I have always contended that the catcher was the most unappreciated man on the diamond.

"The catcher, much more than the pitcher, holds the game in the hollow of his hand," Ray Schalk proclaimed. "The catcher, much more than the pitcher, is the keystone of the baseball arch."

Carlton Fisk, who caught an astounding record of 2,226 games, an instant before receiving another array of bruises. Catcher, said Fisk, is "the Dorian Gray position. On the outside, you look young, but on the inside, you're aging fast. You're afraid one day you'll take off the equipment and discover you've turned to dust."

Yogi Berra, the Yankees' magnificent catcher throughout their years as the greatest dynasty in baseball history, tags out Ted Williams in a 1951 game.

Protecting his aching body for the long season to come, Reds superstar catcher Johnny Bench used his "back-saving stool" when warming up pitchers in spring training. Right: Bench, the matador, in action.

Hall of Famer Johnny Bench, the finest catcher of his era, saw things very similarly more than half a century later. The following is from *Catch You Later*, his 1979 autobiography:

I try to get along personally with pitchers, but the most important thing is to somehow get them to have faith in you in not only receiving but in calling pitches. Pitchers have patterns, and they'll often work you around in order to avoid some pitch. You have to spot that, and if they shake you off, figure out why. If I give a signal that I want, and they keep shaking it off, I'll go out and ask what's the matter. Sometimes the arm is bothering them, the confidence, or whatever, and they'll try to keep from throwing a pitch they need to consistently get hitters out.

There are times when I think I'm right when I call a pitch, and a pitcher keeps shaking me off, so I let him throw it to prove him wrong. Of course, I can be wrong too, so it's important to work pretty closely together. Sometimes a guy will walk out to the mound and I know that he doesn't have a chance, that he doesn't have the stuff. I'll do what I can, start thinking, start working the hitters and keep them off-stride. That is difficult, especially in a year in which we have a lot of veterans out, and new, young pitchers are being asked to start in big games. That can be hard, mentally fatiguing for me. I have to work, change speeds, go to weaknesses, move the ball around. With a Tom Seaver I don't have that pressure. But a Seaver is rare, and a game with a pitcher of his caliber in which a catcher can flash a sign and go with the pitch, is the exception. Most of the time I've got to calculate every pitch and weigh every option.

Johnny Bench, the matador, in action.

In a 1956 article in *The Saturday Evening Post*, three-time National League Most Valuable Player Roy Campanella, star of the Dodgers' unlikely 1955 World Series victory over the mighty Yankees, echoed Schalk's and Bench's words:

An unruffled catcher, one who won't let himself get rattled, means a lot to a team," said Gabby Hartnett, who was famous for his unflappability during a nineteen-year career with the Cubs.

I considered myself the quarterback for Brooklyn's greatest triumph.

That's just what a catcher is. He must know not only what his pitcher can throw but what he's got in any given game or at any given point in a game. To me, there's no such thing as a set book for a hitter, because a pitcher's curve doesn't break the same every day or his fast ball isn't as alive or his control isn't as sharp.

A catcher must know the pitcher's emotional stability, his physical characteristics and his mental capacity. He must know just what the other team can do and what it may want to do. He must know the other manager's philosophy of baseball and his tactics as well as he does his own. He must create, memorize and transmit a set of signs for each of his pitchers, as well as signs for each of his infielders on the chance of a pick-off play on the bases. He must be a combination of coach, conniver and father confessor—or else he's only part of a catcher.

Gabby Hartnett, whose Hall of Fame career with the Chicago Cubs spanned nearly two decades, put it neatly: "A catcher must be a kind of anchor to windward for a ball team."

Not that all the conniving in the world allows the catcher consistently to outguess a slugger of Babe Ruth's talents, though. "What is the best way of fooling Babe Ruth?" Schalk asked. "I frankly refuse to answer that question. It isn't because I have trade secrets which I dislike to expose. I wish I had such secrets, or knew where I could get them. . . . But, after a lot of study and worry and disappointment, I have come to the rather hopeless conclusion that there isn't any way to fool Babe Ruth."

In a way, though, even such unsolvable puzzles, and the effort to solve them, added to the joy of being a catcher, for Schalk at least. When told that many parents were warning their sons to avoid the position—due to its lack of glamour and ever-present risk of injury—Schalk snorted. "Outfielders," he said in disgust. "You have been listening to outfielders. But don't let them ever tell you there is a better job in baseball than catching."

Or, as Hall of Famer Al Lopez, who caught a stunning 1,918 games in a nineteen-year major-league career, said after that career was over: "If I had to do it over again, I would be a catcher again. I would try to catch more games than what I caught, if I had the opportunity."

Overleaf, left:
Colliding with Roy Campanella was like running into Plymouth Rock, as Billy Martin found out during the 1953 World Series.

Overleaf, right:
Roy Campanella chasing a foul pop, a play that Gabby Hartnett called one of the catcher's hardest jobs. "They go a long way up in the air, and when they come down they're traveling fast," Hartnett explained. "Moreover, they don't seem to come just where you expect them sometimes."

90

First Base

Vic Power, a perennial Gold Glove winner, never hit quite well enough for a first baseman for any team to justify keeping him for very long.

First basemen don't often get much respect for their fielding. Think of the dominant figures—the Hall of Famers—at the position, and what comes to mind? Slow-footed, not-very-mobile sluggers who can catch the ball that's thrown to them but who win games by blasting home runs.

Examples: Dan Brouthers, Roger Connor, Lou Gehrig, Hank Greenberg, Harmon Killebrew, Johnny Mize, Bill Terry. It's not that these men couldn't field, but that first base was the best place for them to play while concentrating on their chief skill: murdering the baseball with their bats.

First base also gets a bad rap because it's the place that aging hitters go when their legs don't permit them to play any other position. Ernie Banks, Willie Stargell, and other Hall of Famers played the last years of their career at first.

When a player comes up through the system at another position but then proves not to be able to handle it at the major-league level, he also usually gets moved to first. This happened to Hall of Famer Jimmie Foxx, as he told interviewer Ken Smith: "I played virtually all positions. . . . I played first base more than anything else. I'd never played first base at all until the day the season opened in '29. I was supposed to play third. . . . Mr. Mack came into the clubhouse that morning and said, 'Do you have a first baseman's glove?' I said, 'No sir, I don't.' He said, 'Well, get one, you're playing first today.'"

Of course, even the sluggers had to work hard to learn their position. In 1927's *Secrets of Baseball*, Gehrig offered some fascinating insights:

I've found it a good idea to start fielding practice indoors, on a wooden floor. When I was trying out for the Columbia University team Coach Andy Coakley used to get his men into the gymnasium for the first week of practice, and we threw grounders to each other before they even put up the batting cage. Coach Coakley's scheme was an excellent one for early spring work, before outdoor ball weather had put the turf in playing condition.

The reason a wood floor is good, of course, is because the ball is easier to field. It bounds straight and true on the smooth surface, and it's not apt to make the freak hops you'll get in outdoor work. Learning to handle balls indoors, therefore, gives a player confidence in his fielding ability. Later, when he's on turf or grass, conditions won't be so ideal; but he'll have laid an excellent groundwork in his indoor practice.

When a Lou Gehrig or Harmon Killebrew isn't available, teams might choose a first baseman on his fielding merits. Of course, no team will settle for some .240 singles hitter for more than a few games; the position demands more offense. For example, Vic Power was a lifetime .284 hitter who usually hit more than 10 home runs a year, and also won seven Gold Gloves. Yet his journeyman career took him to eight different teams. His hitting just wasn't enough for a first baseman, so teams were always looking to replace him.

Another example was Dan McGann, who hit .285 and stole as many as 42 bases in a season—yet played on seven different teams in twelve years early in this century. He couldn't stick with one team, even though he was considered a fielding superstar in his time. His fielding skills were so respected that he got the chance to put his name on *How to Play First Base*, a 1907 booklet put out as part of Spalding's Athletic Library.

Lou Gehrig received an education in first-base play while attending Columbia University.

"I know they kid me up in the press stand for running after everything, giving it what they call 'the old college try,'" Lou Gehrig said, "but if I have achieved any success on the diamond it has been because I have been willing to give everything the old college try."

Not surprisingly, in every line of the booklet, McGann emphasizes the importance of a first baseman's fielding skills. "Not more than fifteen years ago there was an idea prevalent among managers in the major leagues that if a ball player were a fair batter and not much of a success at any other place, he might do for first base or right field," he said. Then he added optimistically, "That theory has passed away, like a great many others which have gone out of fashion in base ball in recent years."

Yet there is a tone to McGann's claims that is suspiciously overemphatic, as if even he knew he was preaching to a skeptical audience:

Essentially, first base is not a lazy man's job. . . . It combines the elements of the catcher, the infielder and the outfielder and therefore has its peculiarities, which are not shared by any other position on the field. Some of the greatest ball players in the profession have been first basemen, and so important is the position to the remainder of the team, that it corresponds to the anchor in a bowling team, or to the full back in a foot ball eleven, the man upon whom the most dependence must be placed when the team is in a critical position.

Attributing such defensive importance to first base may have appealed to McGann, but only occasionally is it actually the case. Even rarer is the combination of brilliant defensive with superior offensive skills. In the 1990s, Mark Grace—a steady .300 hitter and agile, sure-handed fielder—represents that combination.

Before back problems crippled his career in the late 1980s, the Yankees' Don Mattingly was an offensive superstar at first base. Still, even after his hitting production began to decline, he fielded his position brilliantly, winning nine Gold Glove awards. "I get a pretty quick jump on a ball, which allows me to play my position deeper," he told *The Sporting News* in 1986. "If a first baseman can play deeper, it enables him to get to more ground balls hit to his right. And that, in turn, lets his second baseman cheat more toward the middle. So, if your first baseman has some mobility, you can cut down on the infield holes at not one, but two positions."

In the mid-1980s, Keith Hernandez put up numbers remarkably similar to Mark Grace's today: Hernandez's typical season with the Cardinals and Mets saw him hitting .300 with 10 or more homers and close to 100 runs batted in.

Hernandez was also widely accepted as the finest fielder at his position, winning eleven Gold Gloves during his seventeen-year career. He revealed a true sense of the defensive possibilities at first base to anyone who ever watched the remarkably aggressive way he played attempted sacrifice bunts—often fielding the ball on the third-base side of the mound and throwing out the lead runner.

In his fascinating 1994 book, *Pure Baseball*, Hernandez dissects how, as a fielder, he would cope with the opposing team's attempt to "swipe" a run through a double steal. This play involves runners on first and third, and usually begins when the runner on first breaks for second. He then gets himself caught in a rundown; while he's being chased by the fielders, the runner on third sneaks home.

According to Hernandez, this play can be stopped only if the catcher lets the runner steal second without a throw—or if the infielders are ready for it:

As a fielder, I feared the double steal for years—botched it royally a couple of times with the Cardinals—until one day early in my tenure with the Mets I realized how I should play it. Once I had the ball in the rundown, I could look at the shortstop's *regular position and see both runners in my peripheral vision, one to the left, one to the right. Holding the ball, I'm on the infield grass and closing the gap between myself and the shortstop, running the base runner toward second base. (The shortstop is the other fielder in this play unless he's playing so deep in the hole against a right-handed pull hitter that he can't get there in time; then it's the second baseman.) I'm "inside" the runner so that he doesn't impede my throw to the shortstop, who is inside too; if I'm working with the second baseman, I'm outside the line because he's coming to the play from that direction. Never throw across the base path because that risks hitting the runner.*

Okay, I'm running the runner toward second base with the runner on third in my peripheral vision. If the runner on third strays as much as twenty feet from the bag, I turn immediately and charge directly at him. If he tries to return to third, I throw to that base on the run. If he bolts for home, I do not *throw home immediately. Remember, he's closer to third base in this scenario. If he breaks for home and I throw to the plate immediately, he'll retreat to third safely. Therefore, when he breaks I run straight at him. If he continues toward home, I throw to the plate. If he stops, I throw to the catcher, who is now running up the third-base line to narrow the distance between himself and the runner. Now the catcher and the third baseman are responsible for executing their rundown play with two throws, preventing the runner who started all this, the guy on first, from rounding second and reaching third himself. And I race behind the catcher to back up the rundown.*

But say the runner on third base stays near third base initially. With the ball, I drive the runner on first almost to the shortstop, toss the ball to my teammate, back up quickly to avoid interference with the runner, stay in the rundown backed up by the pitcher, and key the shortstop to what's happening with the guy on third. If this runner now breaks for the plate—and he's not bluffing, I have to make sure of that—I shout "Home" and point home, and the shortstop throws to the plate. If the runner strays that critical twenty or so feet off the bag but doesn't break, I shout "Run him!" and point at the runner, and the shortstop breaks immediately in that direction. He participates in the rundown on the third-base line the way I would have if the runner had strayed off third when I had the ball.

At some point in this play the runner on third base should make a move because that's the whole point for the offense. The best time for him to do so is exactly when I throw to the shortstop the first time or after the shortstop has the ball and has to rely on the first baseman's instructions. If for some reason the runner on third doesn't break, the shortstop and I execute the rundown between first and second with a maximum of two throws.

With the Mets, Rafael Santana, Tim Teufel, Wally Backman and I had that play down pat. It was one thing we never screwed up, and teams stopped trying the double steal against us.

It's easy to see why.

Keith Hernandez, a brilliant first baseman throughout his career and a master at disrupting the double steal. "He's the best I ever saw," said Hernandez's manager, Davey Johnson.

Middle Infield

Keith Hernandez isn't the only infielder to be fascinated with preventing the double steal that leads to a "stolen" run. For a century now at least, this play has provoked the game's best defensive players to attempt to find solutions. If Hernandez's is the most fundamental, the technique created by the great Chicago second baseman Johnny Evers must stand as the most creative. The following is from *How to Run the Bases* (1908):

It usually occurred, I found, that when there were two men out, with a man on first and one on third, the former would start to steal second. If the catcher threw to second the man on third would race home and the throw was too long from second to get him.

Then the trick of the second baseman running in behind the pitcher on such occasions and stopping the throw and shooting it back to the plate was started. This worked for a while, but then the runner on third got to sticking to the bag, and as a result the man going from first to second would be safe at second.

It seemed to me that there should be some means of getting one of these men and making the third out, so I thought of the plan of running in behind the pitcher just as others had been doing, and then if the runner at third did not try for home I would relay the ball on to second in time to get the runner coming from first. To make this relay one can lose no time, and it would be almost impossible to turn about and throw the ball to the shortstop, who is covering second base.

So with much practice I was able to run in on such plays, thus holding the runner at third, and with a good throw from the catcher I could take the ball and with the same movement pass it between my knees back to second base in time to nab the other runner.

The catcher, of course, must make a good throw for the play to be a success. The ball should reach me just above the knees. [Catcher Johnny] Kling and myself have practiced for hours on this one play, and we have it down now so that it generally works.

Of course, if the man on third tries to get home I am there for a short, quick throw to the plate, which should beat him. I think it is a spectacular play when properly carried out, and there is no doubt it is stopping a score and at the same time getting one of the men out.

It's impossible to be a fan of baseball's rich history and not wish for a time machine to transport one back to the era of Babe Ruth or Mickey Mantle or Ty Cobb. When that time machine is invented, chalk up at least one vote for a visit to Chicago during the first decade of the twentieth century, to see Johnny Evers throw a runner out at second base with a backward toss between his legs.

Evers wasn't alone in being an innovative middle infielder. Second basemen and shortstops throughout baseball's history—from Honus Wagner and Eddie Collins to Pee Wee Reese and Phil Rizzuto to Ryne Sandberg and Ozzie Smith—have almost always managed to be in the right place at the right time on the diamond.

Few middle infielders would trade positions with anyone. "I have my fun in the field," said the Orioles' brilliant second baseman Roberto Alomar in 1996.

Opposite:
"The throw to first is bad and a man has to cover so much ground. It is awful hard on your arm," Honus Wagner griped about playing shortstop— a position he nonetheless manned with evident pleasure and spectacular success for most of his twenty-one major-league years.

White Sox second baseman Eddie Collins (left, with Cincinnati's Heinie Groh at the start of the 1919 World Series) was both a brilliant fielder and a master of infield chatter. "What! Call that baserunning?" Collins would shout. "You look like a goat tied to a post! Say, look at him now; didn't slide, and caught standing up! Hate to soil that nice white uniform, huh?"

Opposite:
With his terrific range, sure hands, and strong arm, Roberto Alomar is a prototypical modern second baseman.

"For me, defense is the priority of my game. You make a diving catch and the other guy is mad. You're laughing."

When Ryne Sandberg joined the Cubs in 1982, he was slotted to play either the outfield or third base. But he was unenthusiastic. "I didn't want to play the outfield. Not enough action out there," he said in 1983. "And I didn't care about third base either. Unless you're actually making a play all you do is stand around."

Sandberg had a fine rookie season as a third baseman. Then, at the start of 1983, the Cubs moved him to second, a position where, in Sandberg's words, "there's more responsibility, more things to think about, more of a challenge." Sandberg rose to the demands of his new position, winning the first of nine Gold Gloves after that 1983 season.

Frequently, fielding superstars attempt to dispense advice to would-be ballplayers. When it comes to the middle infield, though, no matter how clearly the lessons might be presented, they are still frustratingly hard to follow for anyone lacking the seemingly supernatural reflexes, vacuum gloves, and lightning arms of those who play the middle infield.

Kid Gleason, known as a slick fielder during a two-decade career that began in 1888, provided typical instruction to the aspiring second baseman in *How to Play Second Base* (1905):

Throw, throw, throw!
Having done this, still throw.
Then you must field, field, field! And, having done this, practice fielding some more.
Then study combination plays with the shortstop. Then work out awhile with your catcher. Then practice putting the ball on the baserunner. Then stir out and snatch a few pop flies that are just where the blue of heaven is so dazzling you can't see the ball, and where your neck cracks as you run backwards looking for them.
Then for a change, throw, throw, throw!

If this sounds challenging, how about shortstop? Listen to this, from 1915's *How to Play Shortstop*, by Nap Lajoie (who was known, in the words of Hall of Famer Eddie Collins, "for his beauty of form, his grace and ease of movement on a ball field"):

Even the best have to practice, practice, practice. Cleveland's slick-fielding shortstop Lou Boudreau, going over the double play with newly acquired second baseman Joe Gordon in spring training, 1947.

Napoleon Lajoie possessed the required "arm of iron" at shortstop.

The shortstop's life, like the policeman's, is not a happy one. I have played several positions on a baseball team, and I know what I say. Short field covering involves a tremendous responsibility in both receiving hit balls and getting away thrown balls accurately, to say nothing of having to size up a play with two or three possible solutions every five minutes. I thought the sphere of the second baseman was hard enough, but when I tried shortstop in 1904 I found out that I had to accept more chances, cover even more territory and make longer and faster throws. . . .

In the course of time I adjusted myself to the change. I found out, however, that there is one thing above all others that the shortstop must have, and that is the ability to get the ball away from any position and deliver it accurately and fast.

To meet this requirement the fielder must have an arm of iron and must be naturally quick in mind, foot, eye, and hand.

Oh, is that all a middle infielder needs? To Bill Mazeroski, the Pirate second baseman (1956–72) whom many consider to have been the most brilliant ever to field his position, it was. "It's a simple thing," Mazeroski told *Baseball Quarterly* in 1977. "You've got to have your feet ready before you catch the ball and throw it. Most people catch the ball and then take their step to throw. That takes so much time. If you lose a minute part of a second, it's four or five feet [for the runner]. Four or five feet makes or doesn't make the play."

Like Mazeroski, Lou Boudreau, Hall of Fame shortstop for the Cleveland Indians, was renowned for his ability to plant his feet and throw an instant after fielding the ball. "I believe I got that knack of skidding to my right and coming

Alan Trammell and Lou Whitaker, who played side by side in Detroit for more than fifteen years. "There is a special bond," said Trammell (left).

to a sudden stop in my basketball training," said Boudreau. "You have to skid, slide, and stop quickly on the basketball court and it just came natural for me to do the same tricks on the diamond."

Subterfuge borrowed from other sports also helps, according to Hall of Fame second baseman Billy Herman. "The great second basemen of my era would use a head fake or a body fake and make the runner commit himself," Herman told *The Sporting News* in 1964. "They would fake like a halfback before the ball got there, and then the runner would slide in that direction to try to take them out."

The importance of the second baseman and shortstop knowing each other's habits, strengths, and weaknesses was shown by the unparalleled reign of Tiger shortstop Alan Trammell and second baseman Lou Whitaker, who played together from 1977 until 1995. Not surprisingly, the two were thought of as an inseparable unit. "Once one name was used, the other's always came up," Trammell told *USA Today* in 1992. "When I made the throw, I knew where he was. I never had to look up. We're talking split-seconds here, and it helped. There is a special bond."

Maybe, like other aspects of the game, playing shortstop or second base is just one of those imponderables. Future Hall of Fame lock Ozzie Smith certainly seemed to think so. "My fielding is just one of those things," he said in 1985. "I just *do* it."

Third Base

While tradition has long dictated that first base should be the home of a left-handed slugger, and second base and shortstop the domain of speedy glove men, third base has always had more of a split personality. Like first, third base is considered to be a "power" position; if you hope to contend, it is important to get substantial run production from the position, especially if none of the rare run-producing middle infielders (Cal Ripken, Jr., during most of his career, for example) are on your team.

Third is a far more challenging position than first, requiring steel nerves and super-quick reflexes. "Quickness of thought and coolness under fire are the qualities which make a player at third dangerous to the team on the offensive," said Hall of Fame third sacker Jimmy Collins nearly ninety years ago. Added Baltimore's Brooks Robinson, widely thought to be the best fielder at the position in the game's history: "What can I or anybody else tell a major leaguer about picking up a ground ball? You either can or you can't."

Several of the greatest third basemen in baseball history have started at other positions. "I was a catcher up until my senior year in high school," George Brett told the Hall of Fame's Ken Smith during spring training in 1975, early in his career. "My senior year I switched over to shortstop. I played shortstop my first year in pro ball and then they decided I was too slow and did not have enough range and they made me a third baseman, and here I am."

That same spring, Mike Schmidt, also near the beginning of his career, related an almost identical story to Ken Smith:

I was a shortstop most of my life in college and amateur ball in the Dayton area. Played second base in AAA ball. . . . Just started playing third base all the time when I got to the major leagues, as a matter of fact. I still have a few things to learn about the position. I still have a little trouble with my throwing from third to first occasionally and maybe attribute it to as many years as I played up the middle, where I drop down a little bit and get away with a sidearm throw. Third base you can't, and I still have a habit sometimes of not getting on top. That's about the only thing I really have to work on.

Mike Schmidt overcame early shakiness at third base to become a perennial Gold Glove winner.

"The good third baseman has to be alert mentally every minute, so that he can think and move faster than the other fellow,"
Pie Traynor proclaimed.

Of course, both Brett and Schmidt adapted quite well to the demands of third base, compiling spectacular hitting and fine fielding numbers for Kansas City and Philadelphia, respectively.

Yet another Hall of Fame third baseman, Pie Traynor, also began his career at shortstop. A .320 hitter during seventeen years with the Pirates, Traynor was known as the best defensive third baseman in the majors during his tenure. In a 1962 interview with *The Sporting News,* he provided some insights into how he played the game:

Anybody can be a stationary third baseman. But by learning hitters and their habits you can become a roving third baseman. Know the players who are apt to bunt, those who are fast, so you know when you must hurry your throws and those who are slow, so you can take a little extra time.

I've always been an advocate of the school that teaches third basemen to know every pitch that goes to the plate. I always knew it when I played. Know whether it's a curve ball or a fast ball or a change-up. The shortstop can see the catcher's signs and he can relay them to you at third.

There's more to playing third than mastering such fundamentals, of course. The best third basemen also make their own breaks—and Judy Johnson, the Hall of Famer who played his entire career in the Negro Leagues, was a master at doing so by getting inside an opponent's head. He gave a prime example while describing an exhibition game between his Pittsburgh Crawfords and a white team headed by player-manager Leo Durocher. The following is from a 1976 *Baltimore Sun Magazine* interview:

Durocher got to third somehow and started jockeying up and down the line, trying to distract Leroy Matlock, our pitcher. Josh Gibson was catching for us, and we used to put on a little whistle whenever we had a possible pickoff play at third.

Durocher was running up and down the line and I figured he might be thinking about stealing home so I called time and went to the mound to talk to Matlock. "Leroy," I said, loud enough for Durocher to hear me, "if you don't watch out that guy's gonna steal the cover right off the ball." So then I went back to third, shaking my head, you know, and I said to Durocher, "Man, that's the dumbest pitcher we got." At the same time, I'm whistling to Josh.

Matlock stretched and Durocher came down the line. I followed him and then backed up so quick that I was about 2 feet in front of the bag. Josh didn't even bother to get up from the squat position, he just caught the ball, snapped it to me and I slapped it on Durocher. The umpire called him out and Durocher set up an awful racket. "You blind so-and-so," he said to the umpire. "I ain't out." I began to laugh and he looked at me and said, "What the hell's so funny?" And I said, "Nothing, Mr. Durocher, except you're stepping on my foot." He'd made a perfect hook slide right into my ankle.

When out-thinking an opponent isn't possible, how about trying something more blatant? Joe Sewell, star shortstop and third baseman with the Indians and Yankees (1920–33), certainly did, and in the process he was responsible for a change in baseball's official rules, as he told Walter Langford:

Lou Fonseca and I played together in Cleveland for a while. Lou was a good hitter and led the American League one year. But he had a little old trick bunt down the third base line that often worked for a hit. After I went to the Yankees and he went to the White Sox I was playing third base one day against Chicago and to keep Lou from working his little bunt you had to play up close, at least until he had two strikes. Charlie Ruffing was pitching on this day in New York and he got one strike on Fonseca. I moved back just one step, not thinking Lou was aware of it. And as I did he dropped the ball down the third base line.

The ball was rolling along just inside the foul line with pretty good

Negro League superstar Judy Johnson, a brilliant fielder and master at outthinking the opposition. "You got them out the best way you could," he said, "and if that involved a little psychology, well, then, you used it."

Joe Sewell's heads-up play at third base led to a change in the game's rules.

momentum on it. [Catcher] Bill Dickey tried to catch up with the bunt but couldn't, and I knew I had no chance to throw Fonseca out. Ruffing came over to pick up the ball but as he bent over I yelled "Let it roll!" and he did.

I got in front of that ball with my front spikes and scratched a trench across the foul line at a forty-five degree angle. The ball hit that trench and rolled foul, and as soon as it did I grabbed it. Fonseca was already on first base, but old Bill Dineen, the umpire, yelled "Foul ball!" Donie Bush was managing the White Sox then and boy they charged out at old Bill. You never heard such a commotion. I never said a word but just laid back laughing to myself.

So they made Lou go back to the plate and then Charlie Ruffing struck him out. That was the icing on the cake. Lou threw his bat away up in the air and both Dickey and Dineen had to run to keep from getting hit when it came down. Fonseca turned to me and cussed me out with everything in the book. But I never said a word and just kept laughing.

Will Harridge was president of the American League and the next day we were taking hitting practice and Bill Dineen came out and called for me. He said, "Where's Joe? Where's Joe Sewell?" Someone told him I was sitting at one end of the bench and he called to me. I said, "Bill, what in heaven's name have I done now?" He said, "It ain't what you did today, it's what you did yesterday." I said, "What was that?" He said, "You know that canyon you dug down that line and made that ball roll out? Well, that's against the rules today."

What happened was that Dineen had called Harridge and they made a temporary rule, and then the following summer when the rules committee met they put that in the rule book. And it's still in the rule book right now.

What makes a major leaguer a fine fielder is consistency, sprinkled with an occasional highlight-film play. What transforms you into a legend, however, is timing—the ability to surpass yourself in the most important moments of your career. The Pirates' Roberto Clemente did that in the 1971 World Series, playing with such fire and intensity in the field, at bat, and on the basepaths that baseball fans realized that they were witnessing one of the finest players in the history of the game.

A year earlier, it had been Brooks Robinson's turn. Everyone already knew the Orioles' third baseman was perhaps the most brilliant defensive third baseman in the history of baseball (after all, by 1970 he'd been a star for sixteen years), but in the Series that year baseball fans across the world saw it for themselves.

Time and again, Robinson ranged far and wide—sometimes even into foul territory—to snag wicked liners and tricky grounders. It was a spectacular display of reflexes and cool nerves, and (along with Robinson's .429 Series batting average) the main reason the Orioles beat the N.L. champion Cincinnati Reds in five games.

Robinson's exploits left the Reds players gasping in disbelief. "That guy can field a ball with a pair of pliers," Pete Rose exclaimed during the Series. "He plays like his car just has been repossessed," added Reds' second baseman Tommy Helms, guessing (accurately) that Robinson would be awarded the car *Sport* magazine gave to the Series MVP.

Even Robinson realized at the time how special his Series exploits were. "I

Casey Stengel, who had watched third basemen come and go for more than half a century, had a word of advice for any player who came to bat while Brooks Robinson was playing the position: "Don't hit it to that feller."

tell people that I played almost twenty-three years professionally, and I never had five games in a row like I had in that particular World Series," he told ESPN's Roy Firestone later. "It just was a once-in-a-lifetime five-game series and it happened to be the World Series. And the thing people don't remember is that the first ball hit to me in that Series happened to be an error!"

Brooks Robinson robs Johnny Bench—again—in the fifth and final game of the 1970 World Series. "The only way to beat him," sighed Bench, "is to hit it over his head."

Outfield

"I love to play defense because it's just you and the ball."

The man who expressed this emotion is Mariner superstar Ken Griffey, Jr. But would it be surprising if this statement had come from Willie Mays, Roberto Clemente, Richie Ashburn, Tris Speaker, Barry Bonds, or any of the other brilliant players who have graced the outfield since the birth of major-league baseball?

If, as many believe, the triple is the most exciting offensive play in baseball, then the sight of an outfielder racing across the grass in pursuit of a long drive may be its equivalent on defense. But even for those few outfielders with seemingly golden instincts, who never seem to be out of position, who always seem to be on the run toward the ball at the moment it leaves the bat, the truth about outfielding is that it involves hard work and lots of practice.

And not everyone adjusts to it immediately, especially those ballplayers who come up through the minors playing other positions. Casey Stengel, for example, started out as a pitcher before being converted to the outfield. The transition, he told interviewer Ken Smith in 1964, was not smooth:

I had a very hard time for two or three years being an outfielder because I'd only pitched off a pitching rubber which was sixty feet to home plate, and I couldn't catch flies over my head, and I used to back up to try and catch a fly ball like you might say a cow or horse would that was in a stall, they'd back out. I thought I was a great outfielder the first two years, and I found out I wasn't covering very much ground, I was doing it in a backing way.

Mickey Mantle, who played shortstop in the minors ("I was a thorough-going butcher in the infield" was his own assessment), found center field far more to his liking. In his characteristically straightforward *The Education of a Baseball Player*, Mantle describes the hard work that leads to seemingly effortless outfield play: "All you need, to learn how to position yourself so you can handle these balls, is practice. You won't get all you need of that in a ball game, so you have to have someone to hit fungoes to you by the hour."

In *Secrets of Baseball*, Tris Speaker tells of learning a similar lesson:

One of the first things I did after I "came up" to the Boston Red Sox from the minor leagues was chase fungoes from the bat of Cy Young, one of the greatest twirlers who ever threw a baseball.

Young used to have a passion for hitting fungoes whenever he wasn't in fielding practice, or pitching to batters. I think it was the first afternoon I was on the field that he called to me.

"Say, youngster," he shouted, "get out there in the field and catch a few flies."

Out I went, mighty glad of every chance I could get to show the club managers and the other players what I could do. I guess I started by playing pretty deep, for it wasn't long before Young was giving me hints about coming closer to the infield.

"Learn to play in and go back for the longer flies," he advised me. Best advice I ever had. For Young kept hitting fungoes, and I kept developing the close-in style of outfielding. It's a style that's considered mighty effective

"The one that is going to take off and go over your head and the one that is going to drop suddenly far in front of you—these do not look much different when they leave the bat," he said. Yet Mickey Mantle almost always seemed to judge line drives right.

Phillies outfielder Richie Ashburn,
smooth as silk.

Tris Speaker, "the greatest outfielder in the world bar none," in the words of teammate and fellow Hall of Famer Harry Hooper.

nowadays, and every boy who wants to be an outfielder ought to study and practice it.

Or, as Edd Roush, Hall of Fame outfielder with the Cincinnati Reds and other teams, put it: "I always told 'em when they hit to me in the outfield, hit 'em over my head. Anybody can catch 'em coming in. . . . I don't care whether I catch 'em or not, but I know where that ball is coming down when it's hit over my head."

Line drives hit directly at an outfielder are even more difficult to judge, as any baseball fan knows. Even the finest outfielders occasionally misjudge a liner. And even when they judge it correctly, outfielders frequently seem unsure—even nervous—as the line drive approaches, stumbling forward or back, and then catching it with knees buckling.

In *Born to Play Ball*, Willie Mays dealt with these difficult plays:

Two things make line drives hard. One of them is that all line drives—the kind that sail and the kind that sink—behave the same way as they leave the

Willie Mays was renowned as one of the finest outfielders of all time. When asked to rank the best catches he'd ever made, he proclaimed: "I don't compare them. I catch 'em."

bat. And if you wait to gauge them, frequently you're too late, because they don't stay in the air very long. . . .

Generally speaking, your trouble with line drives will be not so much the catching of them as the decision you have to make, in a split second, as to whether the ball can be caught at all. There's no golden formula here to solve this. Even Mickey Mantle frankly confesses he has trouble with "those balls hit right at me."

You can take comfort, though, in a couple of things. One is that the play will be in front of you. Another is that if the ball is hit even slightly to the side, either way, of the line between you and the plate, it will be much easier to gauge.

One thing you will have to overcome, not only on line drives but on other outfield hits as well, is the tendency we all have to start forward, towards the infield, the instant the ball is hit. Some young outfielders fight this to the extent that they go too far the other way and see the ball drop ten or fifteen feet in front of them. But I'd suggest your doing that too. A tendency to move back is easier to correct than a tendency to move in.

Hall of Famer Harry Hooper, who starred for seventeen years with the Red Sox and White Sox, was a fine offensive player and a brilliant fielder. He took his defensive responsibilities very seriously, as he showed in this 1917 *Baseball Magazine* article:

I am an outfielder. That is my profession. I have made a study of it just as I would have made a study of law or medicine had I chosen those subjects for my profession. . . .

Ground covering ability is commonly supposed to indicate speed in an out-fielder and little else. But such ability involves much more than mere speed. In the first place it involves ability to read the batters. The good outfielder

Edd Roush, brilliant flychaser for the Cincinnati Reds.

stations himself in the position where the ball is most likely to go if it is hit. He takes into consideration the individual tendency of the batter, the stage of the game, and sometimes the type of ball which the pitcher is going to use. Ability to lay for a hit comes only through long experience and careful study of opposing players.

Another element of ground covering fully as important as speed or knowledge of the batter is making a quick start. This point I believe is more generally overlooked than any other, by men who are reasonably good outfielders. The outfielder should start on the crack of the bat. If he delays a half second, as he might very well do, he may miss the liner entirely. A half second saved at the start means perhaps fifteen feet of distance. And how many hot drives have you seen that passed just beyond the outstretched fingers of the racing outfielder?

A quick start is none the less valuable, because it is seldom or never recognized by the crowd. I have seen a fast outfielder going at a ten-second clip, make a spectacular run after a ball and miss it by inches. "Well, he made a great play for the ball, anyway," says the crowd. The facts of the case were he did nothing of the kind. He made a very slow start. A slower man playing the ball properly would have caught it easily.

With all the endless hours of practice, all the hard work that goes into being a fine fielder, sometimes even the best have to trust to their skills and just go for the ball. No one in the history of baseball was more spectacular at this, year after year after year, than Pirate great Roberto Clemente.

Anyone who watched Clemente play can conjure up an indelible gallery of images of him in the field. It's impossible to choose just one. Here he is hurtling into the wall as he makes another leaping grab. Here he's picking up a ball in the right-field corner and then throwing it on a line 300, or even 400, feet to nip a runner at second or home. And here he is putting away a fly—one that would have been out of the reach of most outfielders—with a casual basket catch.

Yet, like so many other players, this magnificent outfielder was a man without a position when he was first scouted by the Dodgers' Al Campanis. He had played all over the diamond—even behind the plate—in his native San Juan, Puerto Rico.

But Campanis, who would become the architect of several Dodger championship teams, was no fool when it came to player development. "Campanis put me in the outfield about 400 feet from home plate," Clemente told *The Sporting News* in 1971. "He had me make some throws to the plate and, when I was through, Campanis said, 'Forget any of these other positions, kid. You're an outfielder.'"

Roberto Clemente made countless brilliant plays during his career, but he had a clear sense of which meant the most to him. "A great catch is one that saves the game," he said. "It's just like a home run. It doesn't make any difference if it's a short one or a long one if it wins the game."

Hall of Famer Sam Rice could relate to that sentiment. Rice, who hit .322 in a twenty-year career spent mostly with the Washington Senators, was also a fine fielder. Today, though, he is remembered mainly for a spectacular circus catch he made to save the third game of the 1925 World Series against the Pirates—perhaps the most controversial great catch in baseball history.

In the bottom of the eighth inning, Pittsburgh's Earl Smith sent a long drive toward the center-field bleachers. The speedy Rice galloped after it and caught the ball before tumbling into the stands and out of sight behind the bleacher wall. Moments later he reappeared, clutching the ball triumphantly. Out!

But did he really catch it? Some spectators came forth to say that Rice had in fact lost the ball as he fell into the stands, and that a friendly hometown fan had put it back into his glove. Peppered with questions, Rice refused to talk about the incident. In 1965, though, he wrote a letter describing the incident, sealed it, and left it at the Hall of Fame to be opened after his death.

Sam Rice died in 1974, and a few weeks later Hall of Fame President Paul Kerr opened the letter. Here is what it said:

It was a cold and windy day. The rightfield bleachers were crowded with people in overcoats and wrapped in blankets. The ball was a line drive headed for the bleachers towards right center, so I turned slightly to my right and had the ball in view all the way, going at top speed and about 15 feet from the bleachers jumped as high as I could and backhanded and the ball hit the center of pocket in glove (I had a deathgrip on it). I hit the ground about 5 feet from a barrier about 4 feet high in front of bleacher with all the brakes on but couldn't stop so I tried to jump it to land in the crowd but my feet hit the barrier about a foot from top and I toppled over on my stomach into first row of bleachers. I hit my adams apple on something which sort of knocked me out for a few seconds but [outfielder Earl] McNeely arrived about that time and grabbed me by the shirt and pulled me out. I remember trotting back towards the infield still carrying the ball for about halfway and then tossed it towards the pitcher's mound. (How I have wished many times I had kept it.)

At no time did I lose possession of the ball.

Others might have seen the play differently, but Rice believed that he had reached the pinnacle of an outfielder's achievement: the spectacular, game-saving catch at a crucial moment in the World Series.

Overleaf:
"I get just as big a kick out of making a good play in the field as I do a big hit," said Roberto Clemente. So he must have gotten a lot of kicks, with his 3,000 career hits and innumerable sparkling fielding plays.

his arm without some extra protection, part
I believe in massaging, and advocated it so mu
it to us. If the arm is massaged immediately af
for it. After pitching a game a man ought not
next practice two days after." In Pitching Cour
Phillies and White Sox between 1901 and 1913,
carefully considered advice had a solemn—eve
ing ("masticate every mouthful thoroughly")
night"), and drinking ("a glass of cold water n
the supreme importance of proper breathing: "
form of exercise. Nine out of ten persons are f
have faulty lungs. . . . Stand erect, with the sh
depressed. Now fill up your lungs with fresh a
you can feel it at the very bottom of your lun
always through the nose. A few minutes of thi
and when opportunity offers during the day,
strength. It will keep your blood pure and hol
burns up fat and impurities. Don't neglect it."
or even fifty, times a season for twenty-two yea
his longevity and stamina to staying in condit
as the key to staying healthy during the season

larly on a cold day. He can't be too careful.

to the Bo... pitching ...

touch a ball on the following day, but take the

(1912), Doc White, winner of 189 games for the

...ve an extended lesson on keeping in shape. His

...earful—edge. Among recommendations on eat-

...eeping ("you need nine hours of sleep every

...y be sipped with perfect safety"), White stresses

...s is a most important and frequently neglected

...ty in their breathing and the same proportion

...lders and head well back and the chin slightly

...drawn in through your nose. Draw it in until

...Do this slowly and expel the air gradually—

...at your open bedroom window every morning,

...l show results in increased lung capacity and

...you down to your best weight. Deep breathing

...y Young, who won 511 games by starting forty,

...didn't mention breathing, but he did attribute

...n. Like Ty Cobb, Young saw off-season exercise

...hortly before his death in 1955, Young told The

The Meal Ticket

Listen to star pitchers talk about their craft for more than just a few moments, and you'll soon detect that all share one important characteristic: immense self-confidence. Though some great pitchers are modest and some aren't, all project the unshakable belief that, no matter who they're facing, they will usually come out on top.

If great pitchers don't maintain this indomitable air, they won't stay stars for long. There is no position on any sports field as naked, as exposed, as that of the pitcher. The batter? Not even close. A batter might strike out in a big spot, even look foolish doing so, but then he returns to the anonymity of the dugout until his next chance comes up.

The pitcher who has gotten into trouble, on the other hand, has nowhere to hide. The ball gets thrown back to him by the catcher, and he has to pitch it again, and again, even if he has absolutely nothing and every pitch merely digs a deeper hole and further inflates his ERA. Then, if things get even worse, he must stand on the mound and watch the manager trudge toward him and take the ball, and then he must make the long walk to the clubhouse, knowing he has failed.

And he doesn't even have the chance to redeem himself until the next day (if he's a reliever) or several days hence (if he's a starter).

This scenario has played itself out many times for every great pitcher in the game's history. Not even Sandy Koufax was immune, as he showed when he barely survived a shellacking by the 1962 New York Mets, possibly the worst baseball team of the twentieth century. ("It was the most exciting game I ever pitched in my life," Koufax said bravely.) Yet, to be able to keep such calamities to a minimum—and not to let them affect future performances—takes both great skill and great self-confidence.

Given the stresses inherent in the life of a pitcher, it's not surprising that many show a second emotion: resentment. Pitchers feel that they aren't appreciated as much as great hitters. And it's true: Most fans love offense. They admire a home run far more than they do a perfect inning. In general, they prefer a game that ends 7–5 to one whose final score is 2–1.

This is not an arguable point. Whenever baseball has entered a hitter's era, attendance has boomed. Whenever pitching has dominated, fans have stayed away. It's no accident that the spate of new ballparks built in the 1990s share many features, but one above all: They're hitters' parks.

And pitchers certainly recognize this inequity. "Every year, the odds mount against the pitcher: the mound gets lower, the ball gets livelier, the strike zone shrinks, the designated hitter comes in," complained Gaylord Perry in 1974.

In a 1920 interview with *Baseball Magazine*, the great Walter Johnson noticed the same trend when it came to the fans' response to Babe Ruth at bat: "One of our pitchers, we tried out so many I have really forgotten which one,

121

Kid Nichols, who won 361 games in his career (1890–1906), was famed for his fastball. "In a game a man should never let up in his speed in order to get them over," Nichols said, "for if he does a good hammering is generally the result."

fed a ball to Ruth which broke a little on the outside," he said. "Immediately, the crowd began to hoot and crab. They were mad because they thought he was trying to pass Ruth, when, as a matter of fact, he was trying to make him hit at a bad ball. That merely illustrates what the crowd wants."

Along with feeling underappreciated by crowds that always want to see sluggers slug, pitchers suffer for another reason: They live on the edge. The pitcher has chosen a profession that fills him with worry, with fear—fear of injury, of bad luck, of a sudden and inexplicable loss of control. Every start—every pitch—could be his last.

The history of the game is littered with fine pitchers, potential Hall of Famers even, whose careers have been shattered by sore arms, fractured mechanics, or plain bad luck. In modern-day baseball, every staff in the majors always has a number of pitchers struggling back from bone chips, tendinitis, or surgery for torn rotator cuffs or aneurysms. Even the greatest pitcher knows he owes it all to his pitching arm, and that should it betray him, he'd be out of the majors (or out of baseball entirely) in a heartbeat. That one precious limb is his meal ticket, and a fragile one at that.

So it had better be treated well. In a remarkable number of autobiographies and interviews, star pitchers focus again and again on how best to protect their arm. As long ago as 1901, in an article in the *Boston Post*, Hall of Famer Kid Nichols (winner of 361 games with the Boston Beaneaters and other teams) offered this advice to young pitchers:

Unless, before going into a game, one gets thoroughly warmed up, the muscles become stiffened and soreness results. When not working in the box a pitcher never wants to go around leaving his arm without some extra protection, particularly on a cold day. He can't be too careful.

I believe in massaging, and advocated it so much to the Boston Club that last year, they supplied it to us. If the arm is massaged immediately after pitching a game it's the best thing in the world for it.

After pitching a game a man ought not to touch a ball on the following day, but take the next practice two days after.

In *Pitching Course* (1912), Doc White, winner of 189 games for the Phillies and White Sox between 1901 and 1913, gave an extended lesson on keeping in shape. His carefully considered advice had a solemn—even fearful—edge. Among recommendations on eating ("masticate every mouthful thoroughly"), sleeping ("you need nine hours of sleep every night"), and drinking ("a glass of cold water may be sipped with perfect safety"), White stresses the supreme importance of proper breathing:

This is a most important and frequently neglected form of exercise. Nine out of ten persons are faulty in their breathing and the same proportion have faulty lungs. . . . Stand erect, with the shoulders and head well back and the chin slightly depressed. Now fill up your lungs with fresh air drawn in through your nose. Draw it in until you can feel it at the very bottom of your lungs. Do this slowly and expel the air gradually—always through the nose. A few minutes of this at your open bedroom window every morning, and

when opportunity offers during the day, will show results in increased lung capacity and strength. It will keep your blood pure and hold you down to your best weight. Deep breathing burns up fat and impurities. Don't neglect it.

Cy Young, who won 511 games by starting forty, or even fifty, times a season for twenty-two years, didn't mention breathing, but he did attribute his longevity and stamina to staying in condition. Like Ty Cobb, Young saw off-season exercise as the key to staying healthy during the season. Shortly before his death in 1955, Young told *The Sporting News*:

My arm would get weak and tired at times, but never sore, even though I worked usually with just two days' rest and often with only one. I credited it to my legs and my off-season conditioning.

I ran regularly to keep my legs in shape. In the spring I'd run constantly for three weeks before I ever threw a ball. And I worked hard all winter on my farm, from sunup to sundown, doing chores that not only were good for my legs, but also for my arms and back. Swinging an axe hardens the hands and builds up the shoulders and back. I needed only a dozen pitches to warm up for a ball game.

Warren Spahn, an iron man who won 20 or more games thirteen times for the Braves, sounded many of the same notes in an interview with Ken Smith in 1964, in which he described the three phases an athlete must pass through during spring training.

Number one: he has to report in pretty good condition, at least his weight. If a fellow comes to spring training ten or fifteen pounds overweight, his first obligation is to get rid of the weight. Dieting is the only way I know to lose

If a player wants to be successful, Warren Spahn said, "he has to report in pretty good condition." Spahn, already in game shape in spring training with the Braves, clearly followed his own advice.

Opposite:
Tom Seaver bearing down in 1969. "Pitching can be a very humbling profession," Seaver acknowledged, "and while we strive for perfection, we never fully attain it."

weight, so the human being tires himself, or at least gets himself weak by dieting. Now phase two and three are a little bit tougher for him. For this reason I like to come to spring training at my playing weight, or even lighter.

Now I have two problems: my legs and my arm. Your arm is only as good as your legs are, so this phase is number two and this is the one you have to concentrate on. You're on your legs playing the game, you can feel when your legs aren't in shape because you go to move to your left and you kind of stumble. Your legs aren't strong enough to move that way.

So you have to do the running and moving that are necessary in the game, and by this token you're allowing yourself to throw as we do in baseball without hurting your arm.

"The pitchers must appreciate that they are not any better than their wind, and wind improves with running, with work," added Hall of Famer Herb Pennock, who won 240 games in a career that lasted twenty-two years (1912–34). "You pitch with your legs and your wind just as much as you do with your arm."

Once the season starts, staying in condition is essential. But so is coming up with methods of preventing fatigue and burnout—both of which can lead to injury. In the olden days, pitchers had a way of maintaining strength: They didn't throw as hard as they could on every pitch.

Today, in the era of middle-relief men, set-up specialists, and closers, the idea that a starter would hold anything back is heresy. Earlier this century, though, any pitcher who used his hardest stuff from the start of the game was considered at best green, and at worst dangerously stupid. After all, of the 815 games Cy Young started in his career, he completed 750. (Those may be the least likely baseball records ever to be broken.) Today's best starters, on the other hand, may complete only ten games a season—but they're throwing 90 miles per hour from the first pitch.

Holding back his best stuff worked for Eddie Plank, who won 20 games seven times for the Philadelphia Athletics between 1901 and 1914, on his way to 326 career wins. "Like most youngsters, I started out with the idea that I would have to put all my strength into every pitch," he said. "But I made a study of pitching, and soon discovered that if I went on in this manner I could not last long. I then saved my strength for the critical stages of the game, and now I do not put any more on the ball than I have to."

Other great pitchers of that era were also open about the need for a pitcher to pace himself. "When a man who is a dangerous batter comes up with a runner on third," said Walter Johnson, "you simply turn on more juice."

Today, of course, radar guns chart every pitch hurled by every pitcher—and if they show that a starter consistently throws, say, 88 miles per hour in the first inning and 95 miles per hour in the seventh, he'll be in line for a lecture from his manager or pitching coach. Not to mention that he'd be unlikely even to make it to the seventh—his attempts to save his strength in the early innings would, more often than not, lead to an early shower. Modern pitchers throw hard from the first batter to the last.

This isn't to say that a pitcher throws every pitch in a game with exactly the same intensity. Tom Seaver, the 300-game winner who was also an avid student

After years battling his control, Sandy Koufax established himself as one of the greatest pitchers of all time in 1961. "You think, 'I'm going to do this,' and you can't," Koufax said of his struggles. "But then you do it. There's a whole lot of pleasure in that when you've been wild all your life."

Opposite:
Sandy Koufax finishing up his second of four no-hitters, May 11, 1963. "I was given the ability to throw the ball harder than most people," he said. "Something in my arm is built a little different."

and teacher of his craft, gave an excellent description of situational pitching in his 1984 book, *The Art of Pitching*:

Only three or four outs directly affect the outcome of any given game. Stated another way, a game may ride on just three or four pitches that the pitcher must choose carefully and throw with accuracy. No matter how lopsided the final score, you can usually pinpoint the moment that a key out was made or not made and a vital pitch was thrown or misthrown.

One of the greatest challenges of pitching is to recognize these critical situations and to rise to the occasion with consistency and a competitive spirit. You can train yourself to identify the outs that you must get, and within the bounds of sportsmanship, to go about getting them. You must be like a prize-fighter going after his opponent. Once you have him cornered or hurt, you must keep the pressure on. Make the batter try to go after the pitch you throw, not wait for the pitch he wants.

The goal is, therefore, to give everything you've got on every pitch—but then to give just a little more when facing one of those critical situations. Anyone who has watched baseball will realize that this isn't a contradiction: Somehow, even a pitcher who seems to have been working at peak capacity will rear back and snap off a sharper curve, get more movement on his slider, or add a foot or two to his fastball when it's absolutely necessary. The great pitchers do, at least.

Yet, to Sandy Koufax, there is peril in a pitcher's trying too hard in critical situations. In *Koufax* (1966), the magnificent Dodger left-hander preached the need for control. By this, he didn't mean merely getting the ball over the plate—but staying in command of one's emotions and one's pitches as well.

For Koufax, the revelation came during spring training in 1961, after six seasons of seemingly hopeless battles with the strike zone. Finally mature enough to listen to the advice of others, Koufax decided not to force his fastball—not to try to throw it as hard as possible—whenever he got into trouble on the mound. "I was still throwing as hard as ever," he explains in *Koufax*. "I was just taking the grunt out of it."

The language of baseball makes it very difficult to explain what I was doing differently. Expressions like "reaching back to find something extra" and "never letting up" lead people to think that a pitcher takes a deep breath, closes his eyes, and challenges the batter to a contest of muscle. That isn't it at all. It is desire that is being talked about when they use those expressions. Determination. The trouble comes when the desire and determination are uncontrolled.

The only way I can explain it is to say that the most you can give to anything you are doing is 100 per cent. If you use up that 100 per cent in sheer physical effort, there is nothing left over for thinking. You must therefore apportion some minimum percentage—5 per cent or 10 per cent are good arbitrary, meaningless figures—to thinking about what you are doing. By concentrating on where you want the ball to go, you seem to take the stress out of throwing. You are not pressing, you are not forcing the ball. You are taking nothing out of the physical effort, in other words, except—again—the grunt.

Heat and Movement

Over the years, a variety of different pitches have come in and out of vogue. But from baseball's earliest days, the basic pitch in the repertoire of almost every hurler has been the simplest: the fastball. As Smoky Joe Wood—possessor of a smoking fastball before he hurt his arm—said, most succinctly of all: "Speed, terrific speed, in my opinion, is the greatest essential that any pitcher can possess."

Tom Seaver went into more detail in *The Art of Pitching*, describing a speech he gave to high school and college baseball coaches in 1983:

I decided to start the proceedings with a teaser for the assembled experts. I asked, "What is the most important pitch in baseball?"

I got a lively response. "Slider!" boomed a few voices. "The fastball!" rejoined others. A lover of the high hard one yelled, "Strikeout pitch!" There was a smattering of support for specialty pitches like the forkball and the knuckleball. After listening to the various opinions, I said, "The most important pitch in baseball is the fastball."

I then posed another question. "What is the second most important pitch in baseball?" Everybody had an opinion on that one, with more votes for sliders, curves, change-ups, forkballs. A wise guy in the back even shouted, "Spitter!" After listening for a while, I said, "The second most important pitch in baseball is the fastball."

The fastball is the cornerstone for the foundation of the art of pitching. . . . You cannot possess effective curveballs, sliders, or change-ups if you have not established the pre-eminence of your fastball.

In *Pitching* (1975), Oriole great Jim Palmer concurred. "You can make a mistake with a good fast ball and get away with it, whereas you're not likely to be that lucky making one on another type of pitch," Palmer said. "For instance, a slider is good in only one or possibly two areas—but you can make a mistake and throw a fast ball down the middle of the plate, and *if it moves*, the hitter might pop it up or line it out."

Kid Nichols shared Palmer's opinion on the moving fastball—especially the one that rises, which he called the "jump ball." "That there is such a thing as a jump ball I believe is universally conceded, but like other pitchers I am in the dark as to its cause," he said. "I know this much about it. Speed is the first requirement to obtain it."

In his 1968 autobiography, *From Ghetto to Glory*, Cardinal superstar Bob Gibson shows how if you can combine a rising fastball with one that sinks, you may be on your way to the Hall of Fame:

I discovered, by fooling around on the sidelines in 1961, that I could make my fastball do different things depending on how I held it. When I held it across the seams, as I always did, the ball sailed away from a right-handed hitter. When I held it with the seams, I found that the ball would sink and tail into a right-handed hitter. I discovered this quite by accident. You're always messing around, trying to figure out what you can do with a pitch or how the ball will react to a certain way you hold it.

So I had two fast balls. One—the sailer—is my "out" pitch, the one I get

Bob Gibson put every ounce of himself into every pitch.

most of my strikeouts with. The other—the sinker—I use when the situation calls for a double-play ball. They will usually beat the sinker into the ground.

Of course, no one makes it to the majors with only a fastball. Almost always, a pitcher's second pitch is the curve. And if there are a variety of different fastballs (today, the standard heater and the split-finger fastball are most popular), a glance through the literature of baseball instruction shows that there are nearly countless ways to throw the "outcurve," "inshoot," "fadeaway," "hook," or whatever else you want to call the dazzling array of breaking pitches employed over the years.

Though they are gripped differently, curves are all delivered with a strong downward snap of the wrist as the ball is released. It is the wrist snap that creates the top- or sidespin that causes the ball to drop as it nears the plate.

When the curveball was first introduced, it was the subject of scorn and opprobrium—and also of public doubts that it actually curved at all. "Periodically, somebody pops up with the old argument that a baseball really doesn't curve. That it is an optical illusion," wrote fireballer Bob Feller (who often used a wicked curve as his out pitch) in 1948's *How to Pitch*. "If this is so, I have struck out a great number of hitters with optical illusions."

Still, even those who scorned the curveball knew it was a potent pitch—so

Quietly riding exceptional control and a devastating split-finger fastball, Greg Maddux became the finest pitcher of the 1990s. "A hitter will get, say, 600 at bats over a year," Maddux says. "He may see me only six or seven times out of those 600. I'm not going to do anything or say anything that makes him remember me."

Opposite:

"I struck out ten men in succession before they discovered what I was doing; then there was a grand row," recalled Candy Cummings (left) of the game in which he unveiled his newfangled pitch: the curveball.

effective that, when it was first unveiled in the mid-nineteenth century, fierce arguments erupted as to who had "invented" it. One self-proclaimed candidate was William Arthur "Candy" Cummings, a pitcher for the Brooklyn (N.Y.) Excelsiors, who made sure that his name would be remembered by telling everyone of his invention. He wrote this passage in 1901:

There have been numerous stories printed in regard to who was the first one to pitch a "curve" ball, and some were correct as far as they went; the others were not. Like many other important discoveries, that of the science of curving a baseball was the result of an accident. It seems strange to say that the idle throwing of half a clamshell should have given birth to the idea, but such was the case. Seeing the shell curve to the right or left made me wonder whether I could make a ball do so. If I could, I would have the best end of the game, until others learned how to do it.

In 1867 the Excelsior club went on a trip to Boston to play the Lowell, Tri Mountain, and Harvard clubs, and I went as pitcher, as our regular twirler was sick. I did not notice during the Lowell and Tri Mountain game that I was pitching any differently, but while we were playing Harvard on Jarvis Field, I suddenly realized that I had at last found what I had been working for the past four years, how to curve the ball. It was this way: I noticed that

they were striking at a great many balls which they did not hit, but until Archie Bush, their heaviest batter, came to the bat, I was uncertain what caused it. I pitched him a good ball and was sorry when I did, but to my surprise he missed it and I gave him another and watched it, and as he struck at it I saw it curve away from him, and he missed that one as well.

In fairness to other claimants to the prize of inventor of the curveball, it should be said that Cummings was probably only the most vociferous and persistent of those who took credit. In 1918, *The Sporting News* attempted to establish a chronology of the curve, anointing J. McSweeney of the Mutual Baseball Club as the first to use it, in 1866. Candy Cummings, the article stated flatly, "did not use an out curve previous to 1870."

Whatever. Once it arrived, the curveball "completely revolutionized baseball methods," as *Baseball Magazine* put it in 1905. Pitchers had long known that the best hitters could catch up to even the fastest fastball. But throw a pitch that ducked and swooped, and you could fool them—and also retire them more effectively with your fastball, since they couldn't ever assume it was coming.

Everyone from children on the sandlot to professional athletes rushed to learn the curveball. And many, according to Walter Johnson, suffered from it. "Too many youngsters spoil their arms by trying to throw fancy curves before they have attained sufficient strength," the Big Train said in 1923. "A great many youngsters have an idea that to be great pitchers they have to have more curves than the others. That is a big mistake. Speed comes first. If you haven't the speed, you can't throw the curves."

The sheer quantity of "How to Pitch the Curve" instruction manuals over the years is the best evidence that breaking balls are hard to throw, and often hard for even the finest pitchers to control. Scan the newspaper coverage of Steve Carlton's career, for example, and you'll witness an ongoing battle with the slider, the hard breaking ball that was Carlton's "out" pitch.

Carlton was a promising but unproven left-hander in his first years in the majors. Then, in 1969, he started using the slider, and went 17–11 with a 2.17 ERA for a mediocre Cardinals team. "It was a great pitch for me," Carlton said.

Then, as quickly as it had arrived, the pitch deserted him. "I was getting underneath the slider and releasing it improperly," he recalled of the 1970 season. "It gave me a sore arm before the year was over, so I decided to scrap it." In 1970, Carlton's record plunged to 10–19, and his ERA ballooned to 3.72.

Then, in 1972, Carlton risked using the troublesome pitch again—and blossomed with an amazing 27 victories for a team that won only 59 games. "My slider's a great pitch," he said once more.

At least for a while. In 1973, his record plummeted again, to 13–20—and again the slider was a major culprit. "I haven't been consistent with that pitch," he said during that difficult season. "A lot of times when it hasn't been working, I've had to junk it altogether."

After 1973, Carlton maintained command of the slider and avoided the spectacular ups and downs that characterized his earlier seasons. But if such a roller coaster plagued even a pitcher on his way to 329 career wins and a first-ballot election to the Hall of Fame, is it any wonder that less-talented hurlers spend their careers struggling with their breaking pitches?

Opposite:
Steve Carlton's battles with his slider sometimes lasted whole seasons. "I haven't been consistent with that pitch," he griped after one bad outing. "But do I have to get killed every time I make a mistake?"

Getting the Edge

No pitcher has made it to the majors without at least having a workable fastball and curve—unless he had something else to fool hitters with. One possibility: an odd pitching motion. Many pitchers have stayed in the game far longer than their stuff would ever have allowed, simply by messing up the batter's timing with their odd pitching motions.

Hall of Famer Juan Marichal, for example, had a great fastball, but his amazingly high leg kick and windmill-like motion may have been even more important, since they made it almost impossible for batters to figure out when the ball would leave his hand. Even more tellingly, Luis Tiant won 229 games in the majors without having a blazing fastball. Instead, he substituted a dazzling array of different windups and release points; it is remarkable that batters ever figured out where the pitch was coming from.

Juan Marichal's scythelike windup made batters feel that they were trying to hit a ball pitched by a spider. "Don't go to the mound trying to imitate him," Tom Seaver warned budding young pitchers.

Those rare pitchers who throw sidearm, even almost underhanded, are particularly hard for batters to read. Carl Mays, for one, made his living (and won 207 games) throwing that way. In addition, of the pitchers who usually come over the top, some "drop down" and throw sidearm every once in a while in a crucial situation. David Cone is a current example, while Hall of Famer "Iron Man" Joe McGinnity was an earlier promoter of the technique. In 1908's *How to Pitch*, McGinnity gave a lesson in sidearm pitching, describing a pitch he called the "raise ball":

Like the drop ball, the raise ball is a product, more of the style of delivery, than because of any peculiar motion given to it. It is the heritage of the old days of underhand pitching—when no curves were known—combined with the outcurve of the present day.

Carl Mays's tricky—and dangerous—underhand delivery.

135

Grasp the ball exactly as if about to pitch an outcurve. Instead of swinging the hand over the shoulder, drop the arm and let the ball be delivered from any angle in the vicinity of the knee. If you can start it lower than the knee, and with accuracy, so much the more effective the raise is likely to be.

It is not necessary to use speed. In fact, lack of speed with good control are far better, for it is one of the most difficult deliveries of all for the batter to gauge since he can see the ball floating to him all the way, and yet finds it almost out of the question to estimate its speed so that he can hit it effectively.

Hoyt Wilhelm's knuckleball made him the dominant relief pitcher of the 1950s and early 1960s. "It's not how hard you throw, but how you throw," he said.

A pitch that floats to the plate, tying up the batter who is desperately trying to time his swing? Sounds a lot like the knuckleball, perhaps the oddest and most famous of all trick pitches.

In order to make the knuckler dart and weave unpredictably, the pitcher must be able to dig the tips of his index and middle fingers into the ball—a technique that requires long fingers and great strength. Using this odd grip and a stiff wrist, the pitcher throws so that the ball travels slowly, rarely more than sixty-five miles per hour. It moves toward the plate with no rotation and no spin, breaking this way and that in response to air pressure against the seams.

For the select few pitchers who can master it, the knuckleball is another alternative to blazing speed or a sharp-breaking curve. But, since so few ever learn to throw it effectively, they must contend with the sneaking suspicion—shared by opposing hitters and the media alike—that the knuckleball isn't quite fair: that it isn't, in fact, "real" baseball.

Perhaps the two most successful knuckleball pitchers in baseball history have been Hall of Famers Hoyt Wilhelm and Phil Niekro. Both pitched until they were well into their forties—the knuckler doesn't put nearly as much stress on the arm as do other pitches—and both also had to put up with endless questions about their age and about their bread-and-butter pitch.

"It just happens to be the natural pitch for me and always was," Wilhelm said in 1970, when he was forty-six and in his nineteenth year in the majors. "I probably wouldn't have made the big leagues without it. I certainly wouldn't still be here without it."

Niekro, when he was forty-three, still felt compelled to defend his art as being on same level as, for example, Tom Seaver's: "It's not that throwing the knuckleball is any easier. I put as much effort into it as anybody throwing a fastball. When the game's over, I'm just as tired as anybody else."

One would think, given the array of available pitches, that any major-league pitcher would have enough to choose from, but this of course is not true. Throughout baseball's history, pitchers have always sought that extra edge, something to keep them one step ahead of the finest hitters.

Prior to 1920, they had many options; anything went. If you wanted to throw a spitball, a scuffball, a shine ball, an emery ball, that was fine. Figure out a way to doctor up the ball so it moved in unpredictable ways, and just do it.

Given that the spitball and other "freak" pitches have been illegal for more than three-quarters of a century, it's a bit disconcerting to see how openly they were discussed in early pitching-instruction volumes. But nearly every book prior to 1920 has serious, straightforward advice on how best to fool the batter with foreign substances. Here's an example, from 1908's *Pitching Course*, in

Opposite:
When asked why he threw the knuckleball so often, Phil Niekro replied, "It was the only pitch I could get anybody out with."

Tension and Relief: The Evolution of the Closer

No one—not even a starting pitcher—has a more stress-filled job than the reliever, especially the closer. At least starters have the chance to create their own crises. The closer often must march in and attempt to clean up someone else's mess. And even if the bases are loaded when he makes the trek from bullpen to mound, the closer is the one who will be blamed for losing the game if he allows the winning run to score.

Is it any wonder, then, that future Hall of Fame closer Dennis Eckersley says in Bob Cairns's *Pen Men* (1992): "I've said that I pitch more out of fear than anything else and that's true. If you can't control that or channel that, for your benefit, then you're in trouble. I think fear is a big motivator."

Or, as Rollie Fingers (who saved 341 games in a Hall of Fame career with the Oakland A's and other teams) said in 1982: "You feel like a performer out there. People have paid to see you perform and you don't want to mess up."

Different closers handle the pressure in different ways. For the Kansas City Royals' Dan Quisenberry, the dominant American League reliever of the early and mid-1980s, the release was through constant joking. "Humor is the best way to paralyze myself and prevent worrying," he said in 1981. "Also, I feel funnier after a bad game than a good one. Probably so I can live with the memory of letting down another pitcher, the manager, the pitching coach, the G.M., 35,000 fans and my mom."

Yet all the best relievers—including Eckersley, of course—do channel that pressure, that fear, into success. "I like pressure situations," Rollie Fingers said. "I get pumped up when I'm involved in one."

Today, the role of bullpen closer is one of the most important, and most lucrative, in all of baseball. But it was not always so. Earlier in this century, career relievers were almost always failed starters, used to mop up when a starting pitcher was unable to complete a game for himself. There was no glamour to the role. No one *wanted* to be a full-time reliever.

Instead, the man most likely to enter an important game in relief—a game that was still on the line—was the team's best starter who hadn't started that day. Christy Mathewson, Three-Finger Brown, Ed Walsh, and other Hall of Fame pitchers always relieved at least a few times in crucial spots during a season—and sometimes led the league in saves (though this wasn't an official statistic at the time). In 1908, for example, Mathewson and Brown tied for the league lead in saves, with five.

By the late 1920s and early 1930s, starting pitchers assumed an even more prominent bullpen role on many teams. In 1930, Lefty Grove started 32 games and relieved in another 18, chalking up five wins and nine saves out of the bullpen. In 1936, Dizzy Dean accumulated 11 saves to go along with a pair of wins in 17 relief appearances, in a season in which he also started 34 times.

By the 1920s a few talented pitchers were beginning to spend most of their time in the bullpen, starting games only occasionally. The first to attain true stardom in this role was a Washington pitcher named Fred "Firpo" Marberry, who demonstrated the importance of good relief pitching at a most opportune time: the 1924 World Series, during which he pitched in crucial late-inning situations in game after game.

Fans and the press took notice of Marberry's heroics. "World's series heroes there have been without number, but Washington and the baseball world today acclaim one crowned in a fashion new and strange," crowed *The Washington Post* after one game. "Fred Marberry, six-foot Texan, won the second game of the 1924 post-season baseball classic yesterday on three pitched balls."

But as it turns out, Marberry's manager, Bucky Harris, was about twenty years ahead of his time. Not until the war years—when teams, starved for talent, tried anything to see what worked—did full-time relievers begin to enter games regularly in key situations. The Giants' Ace Adams, the Dodgers' Hugh Casey, and a few others began to fill the role that Marberry had staked out so many years before.

Perhaps the most famous of this generation of relief aces was the Yankees' Joe Page. Typically, Page had been a starter/reliever of little distinction. Like most pitchers of his era, Page wanted to start, and was bitterly disappointed at being "demoted" to the bullpen in 1947 for a game against the Red Sox. "I was in the bullpen warming up, not by choice but by command," he recalled in *My Greatest Baseball Game.* "It was my punishment for flopping as a starter and I was pretty much disgusted with myself."

But on this day, Page was brought in early in a game against the Red Sox and pitched one-hit ball the rest of the way, in a game the Yankees came back to win. Afterwards, Page thought his performance would help convince his manager, the still-innovating Bucky Harris, to give him another chance at a starter's job:

I didn't like the sound of being a "relief pitcher." Sounded like a first cousin to a second-stringer. The next thing I knew, however, I was relieving again and now I started to brood. That is, until Bucky soon called me aside.

"Joe," he said in that easy way of his, "I'm not starting you any more because you're a natural as a reliever. If you're willing to work along with me in that capacity, I believe we can do it." Mr. Harris was talking about the pennant and I told him he could count on me 100 per cent, every day if necessary. I was pretty busy at that, appearing in 56 games and winning 14.

Page also saved 17 games that year, leading the league, and helped the Yankees to a World Series triumph over the Dodgers. Indeed, the 1947 Series made a lasting impression: It finally began to get the message across to hidebound baseball men that having a bullpen ace might be a necessity, not just an option.

In many ways, this Series was seen not as a battle between age-old rival teams, or even as a matchup of Joe DiMaggio's Yankees against Jackie Robinson's Dodgers, but as a contest between Hugh Casey and Joe Page, closers. In almost every game, one or the other came through with brilliant performances in critical situations, culminating in Page's pitching five one-hit innings to nail down the Yankees' Game Seven triumph.

Casey faded quickly after his brilliant 1947 Series, but Page had a couple of other impressive seasons. In 1949, he appeared in 60 games, all in relief, winning 13 and saving 27 more—and finally eclipsing Marberry's twenty-three-year-old record of 22 saves. By this time, the role of the relief specialist was entrenched at last. The exclamation point for the transition was provided by the Phillies' Jim Konstanty, who won the 1950 Most

Oakland closer Rollie Fingers receives teammates' congratulations after nailing down the pennant against the Baltimore Orioles in 1974—the season that would see his A's win their third consecutive World Series.

Valuable Player Award after appearing 74 times (all in relief), winning 16, and saving 22.

Of course, the closer's job has continued to evolve. Two decades ago, a reliever like Goose Gossage or Rollie Fingers might pitch 100 or more innings a season and be brought into many games with the score tied. Today, closers hardly ever pitch more than an inning per appearance—a total of seventy or eighty innings in a season is typical—and almost always come into the game only when their team is ahead and they have the chance at a save.

But not everything has changed. Like Joe Page, some of the greatest relievers of more recent times—including Fingers and Eckersley—began as starting pitchers. And, like Page, not all have been thrilled with the change. "You didn't want to accept going to the bullpen because it wasn't that glorious," Eckersley said of his own feelings at the change.

But, ultimately, for Fingers, Eckersley, and every other successful closer, there is no place they would rather be than out on the mound in a tight game, every night if possible. "I just couldn't stand waiting every four days to pitch," Fingers said. "You want to throw that ball right now."

Burleigh Grimes loading up a spitball.
"What I have in material possessions, the thrills
I've gotten, the wonderful experiences—I owe
to baseball," Grimes said. "And I owe all this
to the fact I learned to throw the spitter."

which spitballer Ed Walsh, a Hall of Famer who won 40 games for the White Sox in 1908, explains how he plies his trade:

With the spitter the ball traverses the distance from the pitcher to the plate without revolving or at most turns over only a very few times. It is unlike the fade-away or the knuckler, however, because it must travel fast, whereas each of those deliveries is a slow ball.

To throw the spitter the pitcher should chew either slippery elm bark or some good variety of gum. Never tobacco.

Before beginning your swing [delivery], moisten liberally a spot on the ball between the seams, as large as may be covered by the first and second fingers of your pitching hand. When you are about to release the ball at the conclusion of your wind-up the moist, slippery spot under your fingers will automatically prevent you from tightly gripping or twisting the ball as it is let go. The ball then travels to the plate as described above. With practice it can be made to break either straight down or down and out to a right-handed batter.

But even while such rational discussions of the spitter were being published, efforts were under way to ban it and other freak pitches as being "unhygienic" and dangerous. It was also thought to be just too difficult for hitters to hit solidly—a concern taken seriously during the "dead ball" era of the first two decades of this century.

As early as 1908, Hall of Fame spitballer Jack Chesbro was complaining about the idea of outlawing the spitball. "It seems to me to be somewhat nonsensical," he said. "It has always been pitched, and always will be, and is not very dangerous to batting, unless a pitcher can exercise complete control over it. I doubt that there is a man living who will ever have the utmost confidence in using it."

Still, by a decade after Chesbro spoke those words, baseball rules committees had begun to put limits on freak deliveries. Then, in 1920, came the beaning death of the popular player Ray Chapman. Although Carl Mays, the pitcher who hit Chapman, apparently didn't throw any of the freak pitches—his underhand delivery was hard for a batter to follow, and Chapman froze as the ball came at him—the death on the field helped lead to enforcement of rules prohibiting doctored balls.

Spitballers at the time complained bitterly about the spitball ban. Ironically, they took an approach opposite to Jack Chesbro's. "It wasn't dangerous at all, if you had control of it, and I had as good control of it as I did a fastball," said Hall of Fame spitballer Red Faber. "I knew just where it was going." Eventually, Faber and a few other spitball specialists were allowed to continue to throw the pitch.

Did this mean that, when these few spitballers retired, the spitter and other freak pitches soon disappeared forever from the diamond? Guess again. To survive, pitchers have always had to adapt—and some adapted by maintaining the newly illegal pitches in their repertoire.

Even today, rumors swirl around pitchers whose pitches break strangely or too much. And every once in a while, a hurler is caught with an emery board, a tack, or some sticky substance in his glove or waistband or on the bill of his cap. He is chastised severely, suspended, and fined . . . but in the next game he pitches, it's strange, but the ball still seems to be acting funny.

Even some pitchers not widely associated with illegal deliveries have used them occasionally. Here's a tale told by Hall of Fame Yankee Whitey Ford in the 1977 book *Whitey and Mickey*. It involves preparations for the 1961 All-Star Game, held in San Francisco, and $200 that Ford and Mickey Mantle owed the Giants' owner, Horace Stoneham:

[Horace] said, "Look, I'll make a deal with you. If you happen to get in the game tomorrow, and you get to pitch to Willie Mays, if you get him out we'll call it even. But if he gets a hit off you, then we'll double it—you owe me four hundred, okay?"

So I went over to Mickey and told him what Horace said, but Mickey wouldn't go for it. No way. He knew that Mays was like 9 for 12 off me lifetime, and he didn't have any reason to think I was going to start getting Willie out now, especially in his own ball park. But I talked him into it, since we had a chance to get out of it without paying Horace anything, and he finally said all right. Now all I had to do was get Willie out.

Sure enough, the next afternoon in Candlestick, there I am starting the All-Star game for the American League, with Warren Spahn pitching for the National. Willie's batting clean-up, and in the first inning I got the first two guys out, but then Roberto Clemente clipped me for a double—and there comes Willie.

Well, I got two strikes on him somehow, and now the money's on the line because I might not get to throw to him again.

So I did the only thing possible under the circumstances: I loaded the ball up real good. You know, I never threw the spitter—well, maybe once or twice when I needed to get a guy out really bad. And sometimes, [Yankee catcher Elston Howard] would help out by rubbing the ball against his shin guards and putting a nice big gouge in it, things like that. But this time, I gave it the old saliva treatment myself and then I threw Willie the biggest spitball you ever saw.

It started out almost at his chest and then it just broke down to the left, like dying when it got to the plate and dropping straight down without any spin. Willie just leaned into it a little and then stared at the ball while it snapped the hell out of sight, and the umpire shot up his right hand for strike three.

Okay, so I struck out Willie Mays. But to this day, people are probably still wondering why Mickey came running in from center field now that the inning was over, clapping his hands over his head and jumping up in the air like we'd just won the World Series—and here it was only the end of the first inning of the All-Star game, and he was going crazy all the way into the dugout. It was a money pitch, that's why, and we'd just saved ourselves four hundred dollars.

Perhaps the most famous pitcher associated with the spitter in the past fifty years was Gaylord Perry, who won more than 300 games and reached the Hall of Fame while preceding every pitch with a dazzling variety of gestures. He

In a scene repeated countless times in a twenty-two-year career, an umpire searched the scene of Gaylord Perry's alleged crime.

would touch the bill of his cap, rub the back of his head, pat the pants on his uniform, fiddle with his jersey. It almost didn't matter whether he threw a spitter or not—he often had batters so bollixed up wondering what he was doing that their timing was thrown off and he could get them out with any pitch he chose.

In 1973, largely in response to Perry's antics, baseball's rules committee began to allow umpires to expel a pitcher merely on suspicion of doctoring the ball. Umpires were no longer required to find a foreign substance on the ball or concealed by the pitcher. Now they were able to watch, for example, Gaylord Perry, and then expel him merely because they *thought* he was throwing an illegal pitch.

Perry was outraged. "I think the new spitter rule is ridiculous," he said at the time. "I'm kind of sorry I didn't get to pitch in the old days, when anything went, but I am glad at least I've been able to do my pitching during a time when a little ingenuity didn't hurt a man any."

Ingenuity—getting an edge on the hitter—doesn't always require the use of a doctored ball. For some pitchers, the edge comes from scaring the batter half to death with a wicked fastball thrown near his head. Carl Mays was one such headhunter, and that was one reason that he was blamed so harshly for the pitch that killed Ray Chapman, regardless of the facts of the incident.

Another famous headhunter was Burleigh Grimes, who won 270 games by intimidating batters. In an interview in the Utica (N.Y.) *Daily Press* in 1980, the eighty-seven-year-old Grimes still wasn't giving an inch. "You've got a weakness, and if it's inside, that's where I'm going to pitch you," he said. "I didn't mind decking guys. I didn't mind anything. You like the ball outside, I'm not going to put it there. You think I'm going to pitch in somebody's alley? And have them knock the hell out of me?

Opposite:
Gaylord Perry going through his pre-pitch routine, which left batters so befuddled it almost didn't matter whether he threw the spitball or not.

142

Beanball vs. Brushback

One of the most valuable weapons at a pitcher's command is the brushback pitch. First let me clear something up. A brushback pitch is not to be confused with a deliberate knockdown. There is a difference. A world of difference.

A deliberate knockdown is when you throw a ball at a hitter's head. You want to knock him down, maybe even hit him. It's a pouting gesture. A guy has been wearing you out and you want to show him you're in the ballgame too. You're not going to stand for that stuff. So you're throwing the ball at his head. Now you know that's no mistake, because there's no way you can miss the plate that far.

I will never knock a hitter down just because he hits me hard. If he hits a home run off me it's because I made a mistake. It's my fault, not his. If I make a mistake why should I pout and take it out on the hitter? If I make a good pitch, nine times out of ten I'm going to get him out.

The only time I will knock a guy down is if my men are getting knocked down. . . .

A brushback pitch, on the other hand, is more common. It's part of a pitcher's strategy. A brushback has its place in baseball. Most people misinterpret its purpose. A brushback is not to scare a hitter or to hit him. It's to make him think.

Normally, it's thrown after a batter gets to leaning out over the plate. If you pitch a guy outside consistently he's going to start leaning. He knows you're going out there and he's going to kill you. So you come in and knock him back off that plate. Now you've got him thinking, "I better not go out there too far," and then you come back with a pitch on the outside corner. The idea is to get him reaching for the ball. When he's reaching, he's not going to hit it good.

One time I was pitching against the Dodgers in the Los Angeles Coliseum, which had a very short left-field fence. I pitched away to Duke Snider because he was a good pull hitter and he reached out and poked it over the left-field fence. The next time he came up, I was still going to pitch him outside. I noticed he began to edge out there after it, so I threw the next pitch tight to brush him back away from the plate. But he was expecting the ball away and he was still leaning and the ball hit him and broke his elbow.

I saw Duke after the game. His arm was in a cast. "I really got it good that time," he said.

I didn't apologize to him. What's the sense in saying I was sorry. He knew I was sorry. He knew I wasn't throwing at him. I was just trying to move him away from the plate, trying to get him to think and not take things for granted up there.

—Lessons from the master: the words of Bob Gibson, in *From Ghetto to Glory.*

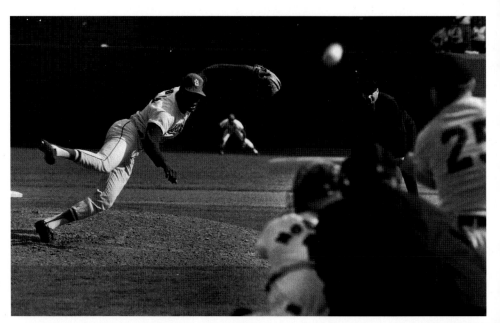

Bob Gibson was a terrifying sight for any batter. "I'm never surprised by anything I do," Gibson said at the peak of his career.

In far more measured tones, Jim Palmer—himself no stranger to pitching inside—expanded on Burleigh Grimes's philosophy in *Pitching*:

Psychology can be a valuable ally of a pitcher. Since it's such a big part of the game, some pitchers will try to psych out a hitter, to work on his mind and possibly develop an emotional edge that's translated into strikes and weak swings and outs.

Some, capitalizing on a batter's natural fear of wildness, will deliberately throw the first pitch over the batter's head to the backstop, or throw the ball well inside. It's true that the batter's fear is a tremendous aid to the pitcher. I've hit very few batters in my career, but I'm aware that just the fact that a hitter knows you can be wild will affect the way he stands at the plate.

Not even Ty Cobb was immune from the willies when he faced the finest fastball pitcher from his era. "Walter Johnson, for a long time, had me buffaloed," he said. "I had a dread amounting almost to positive fear of his fast ball. . . . That accursed fast ball of his used to whistle when it shot past."

Few pitchers in the past thirty years have inspired the same fear-tinged respect as Bob Gibson, whose overpowering fastball, willingness to pitch inside, and aggressive demeanor on the mound gave nightmares to opposing batters for seventeen years. Gibson even refused to warm up to his temporary teammates on the All-Star team. As he told ESPN's Roy Firestone, why should he? "I didn't particularly care for the guy on the other team," Gibson acknowledged. "He was the enemy . . . and the mere fact that we were together at an All-Star game didn't make a big difference to me. And the reason I felt that way was because these guys, two days later, they're going to be trying to beat my brains out. And I always felt—and I still feel today—that when people don't know anything about you they have a tendency to fear you."

Anyone who witnessed the John Kruk–Randy Johnson matchup at the 1993 All-Star Game will also recognize exactly what Palmer and Gibson are talking about. Johnson, the huge left-handed fireballer, was pitching to Kruk (who batted from the left side), and his first pitch sailed over Kruk's head. From then on, Kruk bailed out on every pitch, as if he were trying to take one long step back to the safety of his dugout. His swings were so weak that they barely qualified, and after three of them he walked away from the plate, in obvious relief.

Fear or no fear, trick pitches or simple fastballs, the pitcher uses whatever tools he has available. Each inning, each batter presents a whole new range of challenges, and the finest pitchers treat the ballgame—the twenty-seven outs needed for a win—as an ever-changing puzzle, filled with an almost uncountable array of possible results but requiring intense concentration on every pitch.

In *How to Pitch*, Bob Feller grants some fascinating insights into the workings of a great pitcher's mind. He begins by putting the reader on the pitcher's mound and working through the opposing team's lineup. Then he jumps forward to the game's crucial closing moments:

You are leading 2 to 1 and you are the visiting team. This means that the opposition, the home club, will be playing to tie the score, a thing the road team should never do in the ninth.

Taunted headhunter Burleigh Grimes, on batters who were afraid of the brushback pitch: "If they're scared, why don't they get out of it?"

The catcher, or eighth batter in the lineup, is the lead-off man in the last of the ninth. By this time you are a trifle tired. It has been a hard game on a hot day. Your fastball may have lost its hop and it may be advisable to use your curve more liberally. Use the rosin bag regularly if your hand is sweating. Be more deliberate than ever, conserving your strength.

The catcher singles to open the inning. The pitcher is allowed to bat for himself as he is a good bunter and appears capable of continuing to pitch well if the game is tied.

You try to keep the ball high, where it is difficult to bunt it, but you get it low and he sacrifices the runner to second. The lead-off man, that small fast fellow, is up again.

He represents the winning run and you should be determined to make him hit. You pitch him high and inside, but he hits a blooper into left field for a single, thus putting the tying run on second and the winning run on first. Because it is a pop fly hit, a Texas Leaguer that looks as if it may be caught, the runner holds second.

The next man will not bunt in this situation for there is one out. He will be hitting and you want him to hit it to the right side of the diamond. You pitch away from this left hander; it's a ground ball to short and it is fumbled to fill the bases with one out.

That brings up No. 3 in the batting order, and he's the big right hander who will go for a bad pitch. He's anxious and you stall as much as you can with him, allowing his anxiety to grow.

It might be well to go to breaking stuff, away from this man. A slider could be a good pitch, making sure it's outside. Or, with the game at stake, if you feel that you can call upon reserve strength, throw him a sidearm fast ball, away from him. There is a good chance that he will hit the first pitch and he might foul out such a throw. Let's assume he does, which brings you to the cleanup hitter.

Now you take even more time. You call the catcher out for a conference. You shake off his signs with your head, even though you approve of what he is calling. You work on the batter's nerves.

Start with a bad pitch outside, possibly a slider. He is liable to hit the first one. Try a fast ball in the same spot, being careful not to make it too good. If he gets you 2–0, look for him to be hitting the "cripple," or fast ball which you must try to get over the middle.

You must gamble here. Throw him a curve ball over the middle, then come back with the same pitch. With the count 2–2, you then can go back to the sidearm, pitching away for 3–2.

This brings you to the spot where all of your conditioning, training and will power must be assembled for one mighty pitch. The ball game depends on it.

Your fastball and the customary prayer might be advisable here. Give it all you have and make sure you get a good piece of the plate with it.

He might hit it out of the park, but here is where you must gamble with the knowledge that the law of averages and your teammates are behind you. It's all or nothing.

All or nothing: the life of a pitcher.

Opposite:
Bob Feller. "He had more stuff than anybody," said Ted Williams.

Sam Crawford, superstar teammate of Ty Cob[...]
183 hits in 1915 to bring his total to 2,854. T[...]
the 1916 season saw Crawford manage only 32[...]
a year in which Crawford played only spor[...]
showed in an August article in Baseball Mag[...]
player on the bench happened to mention Pop[...]
brought out that the famous old slugger was th[...]
hits. It seemed a staggering total. I was fairly s[...]
ized in my mind that some day in the far off [...]
sandth hit. I will not say that I deliberately s[...]
feat. It would have been foolish to make any su[...]
baseball. But I will admit that it has been m[...]
three thousand hits. And as the passing of ea[...]
thought more and more upon that particular a[...]
and rap out a good clean drive for a complete s[...]
that little ambition of mine which started mo[...]
think about that ambition now as I stand on [...]
realization. It is all the more unpleasant becau[...]
myself, the ability to realize it." In 1917 Crawf[...]
batting average. This proved to be his final s[...]
dreams, his final career hit total was 2,964.[...]

in the early years of this century, accumulated

ach 3,000 seemed easily within h_____ut

t bats and 92 hits. By midway th_____—

ically—his frustration was mounting, as he

ne: "One July afternoon many years ago some

nson and his remarkable record. The fact was

only player who had ever made three thousand

mped by it. But then and there the idea crystal-

ure I, too, would like to register my three thou-

about to accomplish that seemingly impossible

mental reservation in a game so uncertain as

hief ambition for a good many years to make

season has brought me nearer the goal I have

noon to come when I would meet the ball fairly

e of thirty hundred safeties. . . . And how about

years ago. It is an unpleasant experience to

very verge and cannot see the certainty of its

I have come so near it and because I feel within

amassed only 18 hits in 104 at bats, for a .173

son, which meant that, despite his long-time

single-minded drive to succeed is not always

The Cost of Breaking Records

There is no team sport in which the pressure on an individual to succeed is greater than in baseball. It's not even close. That's because baseball is far and away the most solitary of all team sports. It is, in essence, a game in which nine men (ten in the American League) work separately toward a common goal. Every player talks about playing for the team—but when the pressure is on, the structure of the game brings each one separately into the harsh glare of the spotlight, and then rewards him for his success or punishes him for his failure.

Of course, star players in other sports also face the individual demands of stardom. Michael Jordan is expected to come up big in the NBA championships. Brett Favre will be lambasted if he has a bad game and loses during the NFL playoffs. Once Mark Messier had proven his ability to take teams to the Stanley Cup finals, he was expected to do it every year.

But, still . . . when a pitcher faces a batter at a crucial moment of a big game, it is just two individuals out there, one against the other. Any input from coaches, from the manager, from other teammates pales. One individual will triumph, and the other will fail. That's pressure.

Baseball autobiographies and interviews are infused with an understanding of the often-excruciating demands the game places on its stars. The Hall of Fame pitcher Chief Bender—called "the coolest cucumber I ever saw" by his Philadelphia A's manager, Connie Mack—waited until his career was over to describe the pressure he felt inside. "I was always nervous like anyone else— maybe twice as nervous—only I couldn't let it out," he said. "After I left the A's my nerves got worse. The acid in my stomach made it impossible to eat. I got thinner and thinner."

Even superstars are remarkably open about the stress they labor under, especially when they are discussing the race toward some individual achievement: a lifetime goal of 3,000 career hits, for example, or the race to win a batting championship. Listening to ballplayers talk about the daily struggle that allowed them to reach a milestone—or brought them agonizingly close, but not close enough—and you realize how much they must love the game of baseball, in order to be able to tolerate playing it at all.

For Hall of Famer Goose Goslin, the pressure came on the last day of the 1928 season, when he was battling for the batting crown. As he approached the plate for his final at bat, he recalled later, "I was about two points in front. . . . To win the championship, I had to get on with a walk, get hit by a pitched ball or get a hit."

The first two pitches were called strikes. "I was getting nervous," Goslin said—nervous enough to start an argument with the umpire in hopes of being thrown out of the game and preserving his batting average. Unfortunately, the umpire saw through the hitter's plan and told him to forget it. "I was in a tight spot," Goslin said. But then the opposing pitcher threw one more pitch and Goslin slugged it for a home run, cementing his crown and finishing with a .379 average.

In 1979's *Carew*, Rod Carew gives a chilling account of what it's like to make a run at one of the game's most hallowed marks in our modern, publicity-mad

"I was always nervous," said Philadelphia's Chief Bender—a player who, by all outward appearances, faced the most pressure-filled moments without blinking.

Opposite:
The Kiss of Victory: Tris Speaker receives his mother's congratulations after leading Cleveland to victory over Brooklyn in the 1920 World Series.

151

era. He is discussing 1977, the year he flirted with being the first to hit .400 since Ted Williams posted a .406 average in 1941:

I'm hitting .403 and all hell is breaking loose with the media. Sports Illustrated *and* Time *magazine are planning cover stories on me,* TV Guide *is doing a story. So are* Newsweek *and* People *and* Sport *magazine and* Black Sports. *ABC-TV news is doing a network segment on me. I'm even getting comments on the editorial pages. . . .*

People are calling my house so frequently that I have to change my number every two weeks. Where do they get the number? I stopped answering the phone. [My wife] Marilynn would answer it. There was always somebody calling or ringing the doorbell. At times I couldn't even leave the clubhouse; the crush of people waiting for me was gigantic. . . .

The pressure was beginning to wear on me. It was July, and hot. I much prefer to play in cold weather, strange as it may seem. I'm from the tropics, and most guys from there generally like to play in warm weather because they feel it keeps them looser. Even [Ted] Williams told me he was that way. But I like to hit in 50-degree weather. I guess it makes me move around more to keep warm. Well, the heat of one afternoon made me woozy, and I had to be taken out of a game.

Perhaps all this confusion around me had something to do with it. I don't know. But I remember that I was losing concentration in the field. Like one time there were two outs and a runner on first. A ground ball was hit to me. All I had to do was step on first for the third out. Instead, I threw to second, thinking I'd get a double play. Another time, I was holding the runner on with two outs and a 3–2 count on the left-handed batter. Normally, I would have been playing back in the infield. The batter singled right past me. If I had been in the correct position, it would have been an out.

On July 11, I dropped under .400 for the first time in two weeks.

Rod Carew finished the season with a batting average of .388.

Future Hall of Famer George Brett was renowned throughout his career for playing with evident joy, as if baseball were actually just a game. "I'm not too serious about anything," he said near the end of his career. "I believe you have to enjoy yourself to get the most out of your ability."

But in 1980, the year *he* took a run at the .400 mark, Brett found the relentless day-to-day pressure unavoidable. "It's hard not to think about what I'm hitting," he said midway through the season. "My batting average is in the paper every day, and every time I go up to hit in Royals Stadium it's up there in center field on the scoreboard that's as high as a six-story building."

Brett ended the season batting .390, the highest average since Williams's. The next season, he reflected on the havoc that his intensely public pursuit of .400 had wrought on him. "I took the whole thing too seriously," he said. "I just didn't enjoy myself very much during that last month. . . . I did it to myself."

Even when you do succeed, the sheer enormity of reaching a hallowed level in baseball history makes even the most self-confident ballplayers reflect on the vagaries of fate. In 1941, Ted Williams went into the season's final day—a doubleheader—with his average at .400. He finished the two games having gone

6 for 8, to finish at .406. But, as he told television interviewer Bob Costas, it was no sure thing:

Suppose it had been a lousy day? Wind blowing in a gale, dark, rotten, you know, and I got two line drives caught, and hit one that should have been out, and the guy goes against the fence, and you know now I end up .398. But it was a good day, it was a pretty day, I could see the ball good, and the ball fell in, so you got to be a little bit lucky.

Everything had to go right for Roger Maris as well, in 1961, the year he eclipsed Babe Ruth's 1927 mark of 60 home runs in one season. Maris was not the first contender for Ruth's throne: Both Jimmie Foxx and Hank Greenberg reached 58 in the 1930s.

In a 1939 issue of *Collier's*, Greenberg told of his efforts to make it to 60 the year before:

During August and September, I really tried to hit those four-baggers. With a week to go I only needed two to tie the record. Most people thought I'd make it. I wasn't too sure. I knew the many things there were against it. Here are some of the difficulties the man who eventually breaks it will have to encounter:

To begin with, he'll have to hit a lot of four-baggers in September and that's the hardest time of the year to slap the long ones. First of all, you're tired. You've already played 140 games and that daily pounding has taken its toll. Second, the weather is cooler and the ball is less lively than it is in very warm weather. Third, the sun goes down earlier and the shadows are longer. The ball coming from the pitcher has to pass through the shadow and it is harder to follow. In 1927, the Babe hit seventeen home runs in September. Sure, but I've already said there was only one Babe Ruth and ordinary rules never applied to him.

I didn't feel tired during that final week and I didn't feel tense. But I was tired and the pressure was on me. I realized that when it was all over.

Greenberg hit no homers the last week of that season. In 1961, as he watched Roger Maris's ultimately successful march toward 61, he felt deep empathy for the obvious, excruciating nerves plaguing the Yankee slugger. "What is pressure? It's the tension," Greenberg said. "You fear time is running out. You become impatient. You become paralyzed at the plate. You're so fearful that you're going to swing at a bad pitch, you wind up taking a good one. Then you become so disgusted with yourself you start swinging at the bad pitches."

The stress of pursuing Ruth's record took a horrible toll on Maris. "During the last couple of weeks I was half nuts," he said near the end of the season. "I had splitting headaches, I was smoking twice as much as I normally do and the crowds, the tension, the same questions over and over were driving me out of my mind."

But the most pressure of all must surround any streak that involves consecutive games. The most famous (and undoubtedly most stressful) consecutive-game record must be Joe DiMaggio's amazing 56-game hitting streak in 1941. In

a 1964 interview with Hall of Fame director Ken Smith, DiMaggio showed that he still remembered vividly every single game of the streak, every moment when it seemed like it might be halted.

After going through each at bat of the 57th game—in which he was robbed twice of hits by Cleveland third baseman Ken Keltner—DiMaggio said, "The following day I started another streak. It went on sixteen more games." Then he paused and laughed. "I want to tell you something. I would never have stood that pressure again."

Or as Hall of Famer Zack Wheat said simply once a long hitting streak of his own had ended: "To tell the truth, I am glad it is all over."

Cal Ripken, Jr., faced a different kind of pressure in 1995: the ever-increasing media drumbeat that accompanied his steady approach to Lou Gehrig's streak of 2,130 consecutive games played. But, as he showed both on the field and in his 1997 autobiography, *The Only Way I Know*, Ripken passed that hallowed mark with the same grace and quiet self-confidence that he'd shown in all aspects of his career. In some ways, Ripken said, the day he tied Gehrig's record was even more special than the one that followed, especially for him and his wife, Kelly:

If we couldn't be in contention, second best would be for the Orioles to play well those two nights, at least, and for me to play well, too, and this scenario played out perfectly. It couldn't have played out any better, in fact, beginning in the second inning on September 5 against California, when Chris Hoiles, Jeff Manto, Mark Smith, and Brady Anderson hit solo shots, and the crowd went wild. The streak celebration would have been fun regardless, but I think it helped that the fans had some good baseball on the field to celebrate as well. The players were pumped up, too, by now, and they wanted to perform well before the full houses. And they did. Those four homers set the tone. Then Brady Anderson caught the fly ball that ended the top of the fifth inning—

Cal Ripken and his wife, Kelly, on the day Cal made baseball history.

Joe DiMaggio on June 27, 1941,
with 39 games in a row and counting.

Joe DiMaggio after his 56-game hitting streak was halted. Was his smile just because the Yankees had won, or was he also relieved that the streak's gut-wrenching tension was finally behind him? "I would never have stood that pressure again," he said.

Brady still has that ball—making the game official since we were ahead. I had tied the record. I was back in the dugout for our half of the inning when they cued the John Tesh music and the number 2,130 dropped into place and Camden Yards just exploded. Exploded! In the dugout, there were handshakes and hugs all around and I came out for the first of I don't know how many waves to the crowd. I waved to my parents and Elly and Fred and Billy, and I caught Kelly's eyes, sitting in the box to the left of the dugout.

All of the emotion of the year was wrapped up in these two or three seconds between my wife and me. As I've said, during the baseball season it can be hard for a player's family to get in sync, especially with kids. The guy's playing all over the country and they're at home doing their own thing. But, ironically, maybe all the streak business and preparations and interviews that summer made that part of my job a lot easier. In 1995, baseball brought Kelly and me together and somehow those few seconds of eye contact summed up a season for us.

The next night, Cal Ripken, Jr., simply put his uniform back on, played another game, hit a home run (he'd also hit one in the record-tying game), and broke the Iron Horse's record. In his autobiography, Ripken dismissed those who suggested he take a game off after tying Gehrig's mark:

I told the reporters that I believed sitting down after I had tied Lou Gehrig's mark—one "respectful" suggestion—would dishonor both of us by implying that the record was a purpose and not a by-product of my simple desire to go out and play every day, which had been Gehrig's desire, too. Lou Gehrig would not have wanted me to sit out a game as a show of honor. No athlete would. Take that to the bank.

Someone will break my record one day. Nobody believes me when I say that, but I do believe it, and I want this guy to break the record. I don't want him to tie it.

But sometimes reaching a milestone takes all a player has to give. Lefty Grove struggled along for a couple of seasons after his stuff had deserted him, simply seeking his 300th win. Forty-one years old and an ordinary pitcher in 1941, he won his seventh game of the season—he finally reached his goal—in late July.

Grove was ecstatic, of course, and vowed to continue. "Quit, now?" he shouted in answer to a question in the locker room after the game. "They'll have to cut the uniform off me. I'm going out for another 300. They couldn't be any harder to get than the first 300."

Reality, as ever, had a more sober take on the subject. Grove's 300th win was also his last as a major leaguer.

But at least he reached the grail. Sam Crawford, superstar teammate of Ty Cobb's in the early years of this century, accumulated 183 hits in 1915 to bring his total to 2,854. To reach 3,000 seemed easily within his grasp.

But the 1916 season saw Crawford manage only 322 at bats and 92 hits. By midway through 1917—a year in which Crawford played only sporadically—his frustration was mounting, as he showed in an August article in *Baseball Magazine*:

158

Lefty Grove, winning the 300th and last game of his major-league career, July 25, 1941. "I'm throwing the ball just as hard as I ever did," he said. "It's just not getting there as fast."

One July afternoon many years ago some player on the bench happened to mention Pop Anson and his remarkable record. The fact was brought out that the famous old slugger was the only player who had ever made three thousand hits. It seemed a staggering total. I was fairly swamped by it. But then and there the idea crystalized in my mind that some day in the far off future I, too, would like to register my three thousandth hit.

I will not say that I deliberately set about to accomplish that seemingly impossible feat. It would have been foolish to make any such mental reservation in a game so uncertain as baseball. But I will admit that it has been my chief ambition for a good many years to make three thousand hits. And as the passing of each season has brought me nearer the goal I have thought more and more upon that particular afternoon to come when I would meet the ball fairly and rap out a good clean drive for a complete score of thirty hundred safeties. . . .

And how about that little ambition of mine which started many years ago. It is an unpleasant experience to think about that ambition now as I stand on the very verge and cannot see the certainty of its realization. It is all the more unpleasant because I have come so near it and because I feel within myself, the ability to realize it.

In 1917 Crawford amassed only 18 hits in 104 at bats, for a .173 batting average. This proved to be his final season, which meant that, despite his longtime dreams, his final career hit total was 2,964. The single-minded drive to succeed is not always enough.

Pages 164–165:
Hank Aaron handled his pursuit of Babe Ruth's career record of 714 home runs with typical calmness and grace, despite being under intense pressure from the media and public. "Newsweek called me the most conspicuous figure in sports, and Lord knows I felt like it," Aaron said.

The One and Only Diz

When it comes to dealing with pressure, of course, not all ballplayers are created equal. Some turn gray-faced under the strain of appearing in an important game, while others...well, at least one other seemed to take joy in ratcheting up expectations and provoking the opposition.

That one was Hall of Famer Dizzy Dean, the great Cardinal pitcher who never seemed to think twice before he spoke. Here's a prime example of the Great Dean's style, published in the *St. Louis Post-Dispatch* on October 2, 1934, right after the Cards had survived a tough pennant race with the defending-champion New York Giants and just a day before Diz was to face the Detroit Tigers in his first-ever World Series:

This may look like a tough series to some folks, but it looks like just a breeze to me, and Paul, my brother [also a Cardinal starting pitcher], feels the same way about it. I said, three weeks ago, that if the Giants won the National League pennant they'd be duck soup for the Detroit Tigers, and I meant just that, because why shouldn't I? Hadn't Paul and I beaten the Giants pretty regular. And when the race was over we wound up with 12 victories over the Giants between us, six apiece. And the Tigers should be just as easy for the Cardinals as the Giants would have been for the Tigers.

Of course, I felt all along that we had the best ball club in baseball. We sure knocked the Giants over, winning 13 from them and naturally beating world champions like that kind of made us think pretty well of ourselves. Now we're going to play the Tigers and it's going to be different for the American Leaguers.

We ought to beat them without much trouble. Of course, the series may go five or six games. But more likely if we don't have rain it will be all over in time for the Sunday papers to carry banner lines about the Cardinals being the new champions of the world.

Pressure? The Great Dean laughed in its face! And he backed up his bold words, though the Series wasn't quite the cakewalk he'd predicted. The Cardinals actually found themselves trailing, three games to two (with one loss charged to Dizzy), before Paul pitched nine innings to win Game Six, and Diz followed with nine more of shutout ball the next day. The Cardinals were indeed World Champions, and—as he did so often—Dizzy Dean had put his money where his (never-still) mouth was.

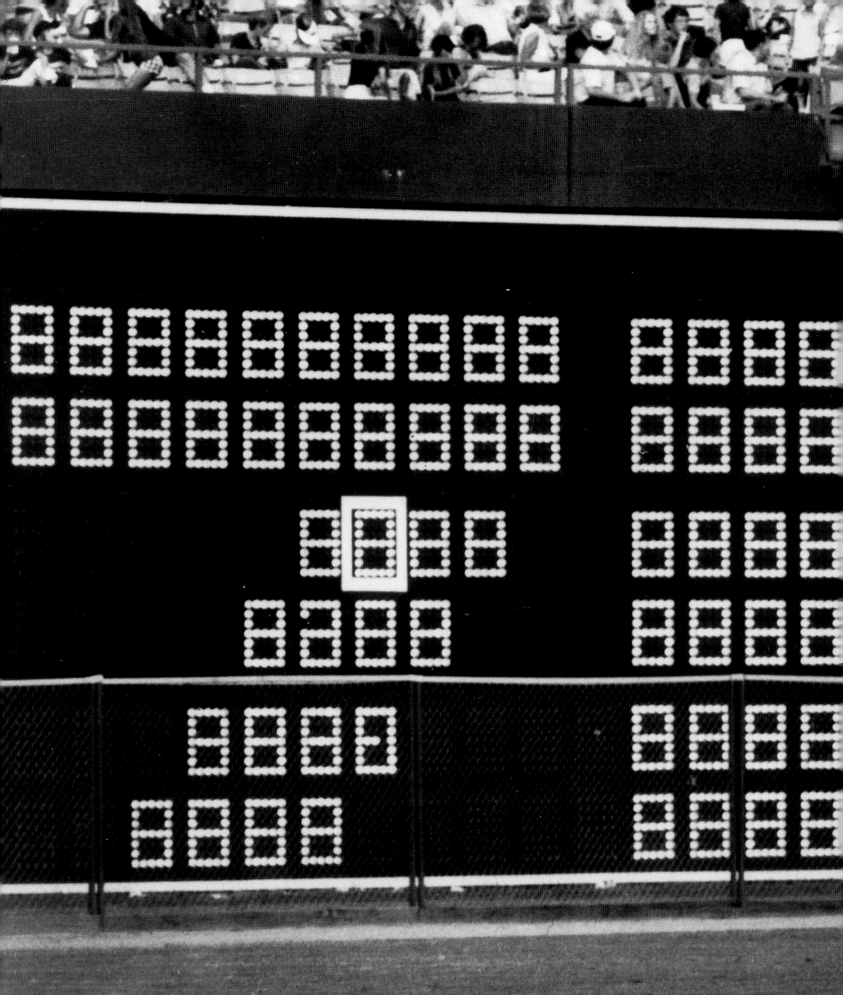

That Perfect Moment

While players reaching personal milestones often tell stories filled with hard work, frayed nerves, and lack of sleep, many also communicate the pure joy of great triumph. Not surprisingly, they often focus on team achievements—the winning of a pennant, or a World Series championship. "It was one of the most exciting games I ever played in," wrote Hall of Famer Willie Keeler, after his Baltimore Orioles defeated Cleveland to win the 1896 Temple Cup, a best-of-seven precursor to the Series. "Afterward, the Temple Cup was filled three times with champagne. It took 17 bottles to fill it each time."

But even within the framework of the team, the concept of the individual prevails: What matters most often seems to be the player learning that he can live up to his image of himself. Most major leaguers have been stars at every level—from the sandlot to the minors—before making the bigs. But most also admit that the final step is the biggest, and that filling the shoes of earlier superstars seems like a huge challenge to even the most talented young players.

Here's the Phillies' Hall of Fame outfielder Richie Ashburn in *My Greatest Baseball Game* (1950):

Opening Day at Shibe Park in 1948 was one I'll never forget, for it wrapped up the dreams of a lifetime in one afternoon. It was my first big league game. I got a thrill even walking into the park, hearing the fans outside say, "There goes Ashburn!"

I felt my fingers tingle as I pulled on my uniform. I walked on air as I went on the field. The big crowd, the large stands, the bands made my blood run hot and cold.

I pinched myself to make sure I was alive, that it wasn't a dream. Ever since I was a little boy I had dreamed and prayed for that moment.

The day before I had been in the hospital. In an exhibition game against Villanova College I had tripped over a spectator, turned a somersault in the air and landed on my neck. I was knocked unconscious. But the doctor patted me on the back, told me it was nothing more than a slight sprain and told me I could play the next day.

Boston was our opponent. Johnny Sain was on the mound. It seemed like a dream . . . me batting against Sain. My knees shook as I went to the plate. It seemed hours before the umpire said, "Play ball." I stepped into the box, watched the first pitch wing its way to the plate and swung.

The ball stung my hands, everything tingled, then I heard the crowd cheer. I had made a hit. When I reached first my heart was beating like a trip hammer.

In the same book, Jackie Robinson said that his greatest thrill "didn't come from any ball I hit, from any base I stole or from any play I made. It came when I heard the national anthem played just before the start of the 1947 World Series, my first World Series."

But then he went on to make an interesting choice for the actual game that meant the most to him—a choice that shows how high a standard some baseball superstars hold themselves to:

His first game in the majors, said Richie Ashburn, "wrapped up the dreams of a lifetime in one afternoon."

I guess the game that gave me the most satisfaction, and was about the greatest game I played in was that one in Shibe Park on August 10, 1949. It was the night I hit the homer off Jim Konstanty. It was the first time I ever got a hit off him. The homer I got won the ball game.

I remember there was a lot of talk about whether Konstanty should have pitched to me or not. There were two out and one man on and first base was open at the time. The score was tied and Konstanty went ahead and pitched to me instead of walking me like a lot of people thought he should have. I think he did right. You don't walk a man intentionally when he's never gotten a hit off you.

We hadn't been going too good against the Phillies. The night before I had picked up a bad bruise on my left heel during a double steal. . . . Right away I knew I had done something to it because it hurt like blazes. I didn't get too much sleep that night and the next day I could hardly put my foot down on the ground. I stayed in there, though, and that night I got a hit in my second trip to the plate off Ken Heintzelman.

In the game I want to tell you about, we got out in front in the first few innings, thanks to the way Carl Furillo was banging the ball, but around the sixth or seventh they came up and tied it. Then they used a pinch hitter for Heintzelman and when the ninth inning came around it was Konstanty, a fellow who looked good against us all year.

It looked like another good night for Konstanty. Pee Wee Reese and Billy Cox were the first two batters and he got them on infield rollers. Then Furillo banged a single into left field, and went to second on Konstanty's bad pick-off throw, if I remember right. That gave me a shot at him.

I don't remember whether it was eight, nine or ten times I had tried to get a hit off Konstanty during the season and couldn't. But that night it was different. I think it was one ball and one strike and then he let me have my best kind of pitch, one just over the letters on my shirt.

I swung, and the next thing I knew, the ball was gone, right into the seats, way out in left field. That's a pretty good carry in Shibe Park. I was glad it was a homer instead of any other kind of hit. My foot was aching so badly I could hardly put any weight on it. I don't know what I'd have done if I had to run at top speed or try to slide.

Konstanty then struck out Hodges, the next batter, but the two runs in that inning gave us the ballgame, because the Phillies couldn't do anything in their half of the ninth. I never got another hit off Konstanty after that but the way things turned out I didn't mind it too much. That fellow may never become a 20-game winning pitcher but I'll never forget him.

The sense that even the greatest players constantly have to prove themselves not just to others, but to themselves, comes through in one superstar anecdote after another. Ty Cobb felt he had to show he belonged in the big leagues every single time he went on the field. He did this by consistently outthinking and outplaying the men he considered the finest players in the game. In this passage, originally published in *The Sporting News* in 1920, he takes on the great first baseman Hal Chase:

Lou Gehrig was the first player in the American League to hit four home runs in a single game. "Home runs, of course, always give a player a real kick," said Gehrig.

No one could slide like Ty Cobb—but he said his favorite baseball moment was a play in which he fooled the opposition by not sliding.

It happened during a game between Detroit and New York. I was on first base with [Claude] Rossman up. I concluded that if Rossman hit the ball any-where except to first base, Chase would figure I would not stop at second, but would continue all the way to third and that he would immediately peg to third to nail me there. I also figured that Chase had informed his third base-man to cover the bag as soon as possible and be ready to take the throw if a situation like this developed.

Rossman hit to the shortstop. I was off with the pitch and did just what Chase figured I would do. There was no chance for a force play at second on me with the lead I had and it was a clear road to third that confronted me, so I barely touched second and dashed for third. The third baseman was stand-ing on the sack, according to instructions, waiting for Chase's throw. I knew he would have me if I slid so I went through with my plans. Instead of slid-ing I ducked behind him, touched the bag and continued home.

The third baseman took the throw and whirled the gloved hand behind him to tag out my sliding body. By the time he discovered there was no sliding body behind him and by the time he found out I was well on my way home and straightened up for the throw to the plate a throw was useless.

The antithesis of Ty Cobb, Lou Gehrig was an ever-cool, ever-quiet player who was both liked and respected by the opposition. During his career, Gehrig was careful not to reveal too much of what went on inside him, but he did open up to the writer Frederick Lieb for an article in a 1935 issue of *Dime Sports Magazine.* The subject was the day in 1932 when Gehrig hit four home runs in a single game, the first time that feat was ever accomplished in the Ameri-can League:

Funny thing about those four homers against the A's. They didn't give me nearly the kick most persons imagined. I was too sore in that game. It was one of those slam-bang games with a lot of scoring. I slapped big [George] Earnshaw for homers in each of my first two times up and helped build up a lead for the Yanks.

Then with two out I muffed a foul fly. It was a fairly hard chance but I should have caught it. Well, as usually happens when you pull an error like that, it was costly. The batter had another chance and he drove out a double which scored two runs and sent the Athletics ahead, 7 to 5. I wasn't thinking about homers or any records when I came to bat again. I was still boiling up over that error which had cost us two runs. So I swung again at Earnshaw and belted him for a third homer. Earnshaw was out when I came up again but that ball still was rankling in my mind. I lashed out a fourth home run. In my last time at bat, I hit one of the hardest drives of the game, but it went to deep left center and Haas, the Philadelphia center fielder, made a great catch. It wasn't until the game was actually salted away that I realized I had performed one of the rarest feats in baseball.

Sometimes an error sparks a great performance; sometimes the motivation is something bigger. When he was only twenty-seven years old, for example, Bob Feller found that the whispers were growing louder: He's had it. He's lost his fastball. The year was 1946, Feller's first full season after returning from service in World War II, which had cost him nearly four years of his career.

In 1963's *My Greatest Day in Baseball* (which includes nearly fifty interviews dating from the early 1940s on), Feller describes feeling resentful of his doubters as he faced the Yankees on April 30:

I suppose the story really opens in the training season. It was to be my first full year after the war. I felt that I was far from the twilight of my career, but it was a fact that from my kid days at home in Iowa, and through six prewar years with the Indians, I had thrown a great number of baseballs at a high rate of speed. At the age of twenty-seven, I couldn't see much point in calling on the full resources of my arm on every pitch. I no longer was anxious to strike out every exhibition game opponent who stepped to the plate.

As a result, my barnstorming performances were not exactly magnificent. I was confident that I'd be ready when the bell rang, but this opinion was not shared unanimously by the reporters who watched me work. From time to time, a critic made tentative motions in the direction of a guess that I no longer could win consistently.

Such comment didn't worry me, and when I shut out the Chicago White Sox, on opening day, 1–0—with the help of a miracle catch by Bob Lemon, then playing center field—I felt that my conditioning methods had been justified.

But Virgil Trucks and his fellow Tigers beat me in my next start, 3 to 2, and Joe Haynes of the White Sox shut us out, 4 to 0, the next time my turn rolled around. That did it, at least for one wire service writer. The readers of hundreds of newspapers from Coast to Coast were told by implication if not by direct statement that they could drop the name of Feller from the list of front-rank pitchers.

I thought that the story was not only premature. I considered it unfair. I was thoroughly angry when I read the piece, but by the time we reached New York on our first eastern trip, my feeling had congealed into an icy determination to let my arm deliver my rebuttal.

Rumors had it that Bob Feller had lost his stuff by the time he started against Joe DiMaggio's Yankees on April 30, 1946. Feller's reply: A no-hit game, which the pitcher called "the greatest of my career."

I wanted to pitch a great game that afternoon of April 30. Of course, I wasn't even dreaming of a no-hitter. No pitcher does—especially when the opposing line-up is composed of such hitters as Joe DiMaggio, Bill Dickey, Joe Gordon, Charley Keller, Tommy Henrich, George Stirnweiss, Nick Etten and Phil Rizzuto.

Yet, remarkably, Feller pitched the first eight innings without allowing a hit. In the top of the ninth, a home run plated the Indians' only run of the game, leaving Feller clinging to a 1–0 lead as he stepped onto the mound:

Only the last of the ninth. Only Stirnweiss, Henrich and DiMaggio, with Keller following if one of them reached base. I looked around at our infielders before I took my wind-up. They were grim and pale with tension. I suddenly was glad that all I had to do was pitch.

Stirnweiss hit a bounder down the first base line, but [Les] Fleming tried to start for first before he had a good grip on the ball. He fumbled for an error. Playing to get back that one run, Henrich sacrificed. Stirnweiss was on second, with DiMaggio swinging calmly as he waited for me to return to the rubber. I don't know how long I pitched to DiMaggio. It seemed to be hours. He fouled off pitch after pitch. The count went to three and two. Then he grounded hard to [Lou] Boudreau, who retired him as Stirnweiss moved to third.

I forgot about Stirnweiss. He wasn't likely to attempt to steal home, with Keller at the plate. Charley didn't put me through the wringer as DiMaggio had done. To this day, I can't tell you which pitch he hit, but it was an early one—and the ball bounced toward big Ray Mack, our second baseman, the same fine infielder who had made the last assist of my first no-hitter six years earlier.

Ray charged the ball and fell to his knees. That could have meant disaster, for the official scorer could hardly have charged him with an error if he had failed to complete the play. But he was up in time to make the stop. Never on any baseball field have I heard a sound so sweet as the thump of his throw in Fleming's glove.

Bob Feller finished the 1946 season with a 26–15 record and 348 strikeouts in 371 innings pitched, proving to everyone (including, undoubtedly, the unnamed wire-service reporter who had criticized him) that he was *not* through.

For the Mets' Tom Seaver, a game he would never forget had a slightly different outcome. In *Baseball Digest*, he told of the events of a July 8, 1969, game against the Cubs, a game that made briefly famous the name of Cubs' outfielder Jimmy Qualls:

There'd never been a crowd like that to see us in Shea Stadium before. There were 60,000 people packed in there that night when I walked out to the mound. My wife Nancy was in the stands and so was my father. He'd come in from the West Coast and came to the ballpark directly from the airport.

I could feel the tension, the excitement, the expectation of the crowd more than I had ever sensed it before. It was stimulating but it also put pressure on me. You couldn't help but feel it.

I was a little concerned when I warmed up because my shoulder felt tight. It took a couple of innings before it loosened up, before the adrenalin started to flow and eased up the shoulder.

Ken Holtzman pitched for the Cubs and we got to him right away. Tommie Agee hit the first pitch for a triple and [Bobby] Pfeil doubled him in. We were ahead, 1–0, after Holtzman had thrown just two pitches.

We scored two more runs in the second inning. I drove in one of them with a double. We got another run in the seventh when Cleon Jones hit a home run to make it 4–0.

Meanwhile I was retiring the Cubs in order, inning after inning. The shoulder that had felt stiff when the game started felt just great. I was throwing harder than I'd ever thrown. I struck out five of the first six Cubs I faced, and when they hit the ball they hit it at somebody.

You try to isolate yourself from the crowd noise during a ball game, to retain your concentration, but as the game continued it got harder and harder to do. By the seventh inning the crowd was cheering every pitch. With every out they were standing up and giving me an ovation.

When Williams went out to end the Cub seventh he was the 21st Cub batter I'd retired in order. I hadn't walked a man. I had a perfect game going. Everybody in the ball park knew it. Nobody on our bench said a word to me but I knew what was going on. How could I help not knowing?

Santo. Banks. Al Spangler. They all went out in the eighth. With every out the crowd roared, 60,000 people yelling, cheering me, pulling for me to pitch a perfect game. Three outs to go. I felt I could do it.

The hitters in the ninth were Hundley, Qualls, then a pinch hitter for the pitcher. When I went out to the mound, I heard a roar greater than the ones before. Everyone was standing up, cheering.

Hundley squared away to bunt. He laid it down but I got off the mound quickly and threw him out. Just two outs to go!

Qualls stepped in, a left-handed hitter. The first time up he'd hit a fastball to the warning track in right field. The next time he'd hit a curveball very sharply to first base. I was trying different pitches on him, but he seemed to get a piece of everything.

This time I tried to pitch him away, with a fastball. The ball didn't sink. It stayed up and Qualls got the bat on it. He hit a line drive to the gap between Tommie Agee in center and Jones in left. It fell for a single.

Disappointed? Of course I was, at the moment. I'd like to have pitched a perfect game. Anybody would.

But I got the next two batters out. Smith then Kessinger and the game was over, a one-hitter. We'd won, 4–0.

When I walked from the dugout through the tunnel toward the locker room I saw Nancy. She had tears in her eyes. "What are you crying for?" I said. "We won, 4–0."

I still feel the same way. Regrets? How can you have regrets about a one-hitter you pitched in the middle of a pennant race?

Seaver wasn't the only pitcher to be intensely proud of an "imperfect" game. Bob Feller, talking about his three no-hitters after his career was over, said that the '46 game against the Yankees was the only one in which he'd actually had terrific stuff. On the other hand, he called a '46 one-hitter (the only hit a bloop single) "the best game I ever pitched." Then he added, "No, the plain fact is that you have to have everything going for you on a single day—especially Lady Luck—to pitch a no-hitter."

Despite pitching a record seven no-hitters in his career, Nolan Ryan also thought often about the ones that got away. "You never set out to throw no-hitters, but you sure start thinking about them late in the game. And when one slips away you rehash every pitch, thinking about the might-have-beens," he said in his 1992 autobiography, *Miracle Man*. "I've had nineteen games in my career when I allowed one hit or less, and when I think how close I came to no-hitters in all those one-hitters, I wonder where the no-hit record might be but for one pitch or one bad break."

Overleaf:
Tom Seaver on his way to his "imperfect game" —the 1969 gem against the Cubs that was spoiled by a lone ninth-inning single. "How can you have regrets about a one-hitter you pitched in the middle of a pennant race?" Seaver asked when the game was over.

The Top of the Mountain

For obvious reasons, players' most memorable performances usually occur in a game that really means something: a pennant-clincher, an All-Star game, and above all, the World Series. "A World's Series is a big event, the biggest of them all," Babe Ruth said in a 1921 *Baseball Magazine* interview. "If you are in it, you are in the center of things, if you are not, you are a rank outsider."

When he gave that interview, Ruth was just completing his third consecutive record-shattering season as a home-run threat unlike any seen before; he would finish the 1921 season with 59. Therefore, it's unsurprising that, when asked to identify the peak experience of his career, Ruth responded, "I suppose I have taken more real pride in breaking the home run record than anything else I ever did. At least breaking that record has brought me most of my press notices and I have found that press notices mean bread and butter and pork chops and other things."

But then, as he continued to talk, Ruth grew thoughtful and brought up another accomplishment that he valued nearly as highly:

Next to my home run record, I take the greatest pride in my World's Series showing [with Boston]. I was a pitcher in those days and I think a pretty good one, if I do say it myself. If I wasn't good, I was certainly lucky and that amounts to the same thing. I pitched in three games in two different World's Series and I won all of them. This is not a bad record in itself for I can tell the world it's no cinch winning a World's Series game. But the best thing about it from the standpoint of records was the shut-out innings I pitched. Stretching my record from one season to another, I worked twenty-nine innings without allowing a run to be scored against me. . . .

There is one thing better than knocking a home run, although I am supposed to like that more than anything else. That one thing is pitching and winning a World's Series game. That's the truth. I would rather stand out there on the slab and hurl my club to victory in the Big Series than to make even two circuit clouts with the bases full. Pitching is half, maybe three-quarters, in a World's Series and the man who can toe the slab and deliver the goods, is the big noise and deserves to be. . . .

There's a satisfaction in standing out there in the center of the diamond and fooling the batters, perhaps burning them past in front of their noses, that you can't get in any other way. I miss it.

But none of us can have just what he wants, I suppose. You can't be a pitcher and an outfielder at the same time and do yourself justice. So I am an outfielder for I am worth more to the club there than in the pitcher's box and maybe it's just as well. For there is one thing coming to me that I didn't get when I was a World's Series player. I never knocked a home run in those Big Games. The nearest I came to it was a three bagger against Lefty Tyler in Boston which about broke up the game. So I can look forward to some other Series, which I hope won't be very long coming, when I can catch one just right and lift it into the bleachers. I suppose that seems like foolish day dreaming. Maybe I am more likely to strike out with the bases full instead. But when I remember some of the day dreams I had at St. Mary's [his childhood boarding school] and how far off they seemed and unlikely, and still came true, nothing seems impossible to me now.

In fact, Ruth played outfield in thirty-five World Series games with the Yankees and caught fifteen pitches "just right" for home runs. So it would be easy to see his nostalgia for pitching in 1921 as just a by-product of his youth and his recent transition to full-time outfield play. Later, he would have so many batting highlights to choose from: his 60th home run in 1927, his .342 career batting average, his astonishing total of 714 home runs.

But . . . in a radio interview just days before his death in 1948, Ruth was asked again what he thought was the single greatest achievement of his career. His answer: the 29 consecutive shutout innings he had pitched in World Series play, for the Boston Red Sox, a lifetime earlier.

While Ruth had plenty of chances to make his daydream come true, a remarkable number of great ballplayers never (or almost never) make it to the big event. Ernie Banks, Rod Carew, Harry Heilman, Ferguson Jenkins, and Phil Niekro played for a total of ninety-six seasons without ever appearing in a World Series game. Ted Williams made it to the Series, in 1946 (his Red Sox lost), then played until 1960 without getting another chance. Juan Marichal pitched four innings in a 1962 Series game, his only appearance during his career. Willie McCovey went 3–15 in that same Series, and played eighteen more years without a second opportunity. Even the great Ty Cobb, who made it to the Series three times in the first five years he played, went on to labor for nineteen more years without appearing in another.

For other stars, a Series appearance comes so late in their career that by the time it does they have almost given up hope. Walter Johnson, for example, joined the Washington Nationals in 1907. Between 1910 and 1919, he posted won-lost records of 25–17, 25–13, 32–12, 36–7, 28–18, 27–13, 25–20, 23–16, 23–13, and 20–14—yet his team finished seventh, seventh, second, second, third, fourth, seventh, fifth, third, and seventh. After that, age and an enormous number of innings pitched began to catch up with the Big Train, and his records became spottier (8–10, 17–14, 15–16, 17–12). Nor did his teammates take up the slack and carry the Nationals to first place.

Just in from Weiser, Idaho, a Washington rookie named Walter Johnson. After losing his first major-league game, Johnson recalled, "I was so confused I even missed the bus back to the hotel . . . and was walking there in my uniform when some fans give me a lift."

Left and opposite:
Babe Ruth as he wanted to be remembered and as he is remembered. "There is one thing better than knocking a home run," said the Babe. "That one thing is pitching and winning a World's Series game."

Not until 1924, when Johnson was thirty-six years old and in his eighteenth season, did everything finally come together. Led by Johnson's 23–7 record and the offensive production of Sam Rice, Goose Goslin, and others, the Nationals finished with a record of 92–62, barely ahead of Babe Ruth's powerful—but not yet dynastic—Yankees.

The Nationals faced the New York Giants in the 1924 World Series. Johnson, who had waited so long, pitched well in the first game, losing in twelve innings, then pitched less well in Game Five and lost again. In *My Greatest Day in Baseball*, he told of his next appearance, the biggest game of his career:

This won't be very original, I'm afraid, because there couldn't be a bigger day for me than the one everybody knows about . . . October 10, 1924, in the last game of my first World Series. . . .

I'd been beaten in New York for the second time by the Giants and I'll admit when I got on the train to Washington, where we were to play the seventh game, there were tears in my eyes. I was carrying my youngest boy on my shoulder and trying not to speak to people when [owner] Clark Griffith put a hand on my arm. "Don't think about it anymore, Walter," he told me. "You're a great pitcher. We all know it.

"Now tonight when we get home don't stand around the box offices buying seats for friends or shaking hands with people who feel sorry for you. I've seen many a fast ball shaken right out of a pitcher's hand. Go home and get to bed early . . . we may need you tomorrow." I told him I would.

You can imagine how "red hot" Washington was next day . . . the last game of its first World Series coming up. Thirty-five thousand people were crammed into our park. President Coolidge was there. I made myself as inconspicuous as possible on the bench, because I didn't want any sympathy . . . and I didn't even want [manager Bucky] Harris to think of me in a jam. Well, "Bucky" started Curley Ogden but pretty soon George Mogridge was in there and then "Firpo" Marberry, our big relief ace.

Johnson in the 1924 Series: Two heartbreaking losses—and then the win that gave him the greatest thrill of his career.

there and then "Firpo" Marberry, our big relief ace.

We were all tied up in the ninth when I came in. I'll always believe that Harris gambled on me because of sentiment, but he said no. He just told me: "You're the best we got, Walter . . . we've got to win or lose with you." So I walked out there and it seemed to me the smoke from the stands was so thick on the field that nobody could see me. I remembered thinking: "I'll need the breaks" and if I didn't actually pray, I sort of was thinking along those lines.

I was in trouble in every inning. After getting Fred Lind-

Walter Johnson in 1924, on the verge of appearing in his first World Series. "I guess you'd call it a piece of every day for 18 years," Johnson said of his feelings at finally making the Series, "and it didn't look like I'd ever see it come around."

strom in the ninth, Frank Frisch hit a fast ball to right center for three bases. We decided to pass Ross Young and then I struck out George Kelly and "Irish" Meusel grounded to third. In the 10th I walked "Hack" Wilson and then, after striking out Travis Jackson, I was lucky enough to grab a drive by ol' Hank Gowdy and turn it into a double play.

Heinie Groh batted for Hugh McQuillan, the Giant pitcher, in the 11th and singled. Lindstrom bunted him along. I fanned Frisch, this time, on an outside pitch and once more passed Young. Kelly struck out again.

They kept after me, though. Meusel singled in the 12th, but I'd settled down to believe, by then, that maybe this was my day and I got the next three hitters. I'd tried to win my own game in the 10th with a long ball to the wall, but Wilson pulled it down. So I was up again in the 12th when it was getting pretty dark. "Muddy" Ruel had lifted a pop foul to Gowdy, who lost it, and on the next pitch Ruel hit past third for two bases. Then I sent an easy grounder *to short . . . and Jackson fumbled. We all sat there staring at Earl McNeely as he hit an easy grounder to Lindstrom.*

The ball never touched Fred. It hit a pebble and arched over his head into safe territory. I could feel tears smarting in my eyes as Ruel came home with the winning run. I'd won. We'd won. I felt so happy that it didn't seem real. They told me in the clubhouse that President Coolidge kept watching me all the way into the clubhouse and I remember somebody yelling: "I bet Cal'd like to change places with you right now, Walter."

A long time later Mrs. Johnson and I slipped away to a quiet little restaurant where I used to eat on Vermont Avenue, in Washington, and do you know that before we were through with our dinner 200 telegrams had been delivered there. I never thought so many people were pulling for me to win, because the Giants were pretty popular. When we packed up and went home to Kansas we had three trunks full of letters from fans all over the world.

For New York Yankee Reggie Jackson in 1977, the ticking clock wasn't the imminent end of his career without a World Series ring. Jackson had already been part of the Oakland A's team that won three straight championships starting in 1972. He was after something perhaps even more elusive: redemption at home, in front of the fans and the Yankees' owner, George Steinbrenner.

Jackson had just come to the Yanks at the start of the 1977 season, and it had been a stormy—and highly publicized—spring and summer. Jackson had battled with Steinbrenner, with manager Billy Martin, with teammates, and with fans. Despite it all, he had a terrific season, batting .286 with 32 home runs and 110 RBI, and the Yankees won the A.L. East.

Then came the playoffs. Jackson went 1–14 in the first four games of the best-of-five series against the Kansas City Royals—and Billy Martin chose to bench him for Game Five. Seething, Jackson kept his temper, and came through with an RBI pinch single to help the Yankees win and advance to the Series against the Dodgers.

After the first five games of the Series (the Yanks led, three games to two), Jackson had six hits, including a couple of home runs. He was having a good, solid Series, helping the team approach its first championship in fifteen years. Then came Game Six.

In his 1984 autobiography, *Reggie*, Jackson said that as soon as he began to take batting practice that day, he realized that this had a chance to be a special game. "The baseball looked like a volleyball to me," he said.

By the time the game started, I hadn't spilled any of my adrenaline. Still had a full tank. Still felt pumped up. Even when [Burt] Hooton walked me on four straight pitches, I wasn't deflated. I still felt good. I was going to be ready when he threw me a strike.

He threw me a strike in the fourth. First pitch to me. Nobody out. Thurman [Munson] on first. I figured Hooton would try to pitch me up and in. That's always been the book on me. Get it up and in. Don't let me extend my arms. Well, Hooton got it up, but not in far enough. I got it. I got it a little on the end of the bat, but I got it. It was a line drive to right, and the only thing I was worried about was that it might not stay up long enough. It did. We were ahead 4–3.

One.

I was still in batting practice; that is exactly the way I felt. When I came up in the fifth, after we'd scored a couple more times, Hooton was out of the game and Elias Sosa, another right-hander, came in to pitch to me. I stood there next to the plate and watched him warm up and I was thinking, "Please, God, let him hurry up and finish warming up so I don't lose this feeling I have." When he was done, I purposely got into the batter's box late so he didn't see where I was standing. I didn't want him to see where I was standing and start thinking; I just wanted him to throw a strike on the first pitch, try to get ahead.

He threw me a fastball right down Broadway. I call them mattress pitches because if you're feeling right you can lay all over 'em. This was the hardest ball I hit that night, a screaming line drive into right. The one off Hooton worried me because I'd hit it on the end of the bat. The one off Sosa worried me because it was hit so hard I was afraid it might dip short of the stands.

It didn't.

Two.

The crowd really started to come alive then. "REG-gie! REG-gie!" they chanted. We were winning the game that could give us the first Yankee world championship since 1962. It was only the fifth inning. I had swung the bat just twice, and I already had two dingers. The people in the Stadium knew there was a chance to be some history.

"REG-gie! REG-gie!"

Finally it was the bottom of the eighth. We were ahead 7–4.

Tommy Lasorda, the Dodger manager, had brought [Charlie] Hough, a knuckleballer, in to pitch. I stood watching him warm up, and I wanted to yell over to Lasorda, who I like, and say, "Tommy, don't you know how I love to hit knucklers?"

On the first pitch if he got it anywhere near the plate, I knew I'd have a good pass at it. The crowd was insane with noise as I dug in. They were expecting a home run. They wanted a home run. They were chanting "REG-gie." Sometimes if you focus in on crowd noise too much it can be distracting. Didn't matter this night. A plane landing in center field wouldn't have mattered this night.

I just wanted Charlie Hough to throw me one damn knuckleball. I had nothing to lose. Even if I struck out, I had nothing to lose.

Hough threw me a knuckler. Didn't knuckle. I crushed it nearly 500 feet into the black, those beautiful empty black seats in dead center. I found out later that I was only the second man ever to do that in the new Yankee Stadium.

That wouldn't have mattered a whole lot to me if I'd known at the time. As I began to move around the bases, I felt so . . . vindicated. Completely vindicated.

Expectations. Fear of failure. The ticking clock. Vindication. These are the factors that drive the greatest of the great baseball players to surprise even themselves.

*Reggie Jackson in 1977, in the midst
of one of the greatest World Series
performances of all time.*

Hall of Famer Napoleon Lajoie (nicknamed "L

exist: "There is no such thing as a batting slum

the way it goes: I go up and hit the ball. The fie

the bench for me. I go up again. Hit the ball har

man out in center goes crazy with the heat. R

catches it on his thumb. I get that handed to

say: 'What's the matter with Larry? Not a hit

hard as ever, but the luck of the game is again

and some guy in the field runs under it too fa

'Well, Larry is getting his batting eye back aga

the plate. I get my eye on the ball and paste it

goes after it finds his arm half an inch too sh

come in, and Larry gets credit for it all. Great

close to himself, and had grown half an inch m

everybody would have said, 'See, the old bonehe

for you. It's the luck of the game." Sometimes

beyond typical boundaries, and the struggling

have vanished for good. Rube Marquard, star

this century, found that his extended slump ca

during his first two full years in the majors.

struggles came after a sparkling stint in the m

y") simply refused to acknowledge that slumps

It's just the luck of th   is

r goes after it. He jus   to

Same thing. I go up again and hit the ball. That

s three miles, jumps twelve feet in the air and

for three or four days, and the people begin to

three days.' Now, I am hitting that ball just as

ne; that's all. The next day I go up and swat it,

nd I get around to second, and some fans say,

' Then, again. The bases are filled. I walk up to

rd. It sails out on a line, and the infielder who

. The ball keeps rolling, and two or three runs

ter! Now, if that infielder had not stood quite so

e of arm, the side would have been retired, and

hit right into someone's hands.' That's baseball

or inexplicable reasons, a slump stretches on

layer joins the fans in wondering if his skills

cher with the Giants and other teams early in

e at the worst possible time: In 1909 and 1910,

acerbating his problems was the fact that his

ors that led to his signing with the Giants for

The career of every great ballplayer contains at least a scattering—and often a flood—of moments of pure joy and utter fulfillment. When that career is over, it's easy to focus on those moments, which can culminate in that greatest of all honors, induction into the Hall of Fame.

But take a longer view, and the arc of a ballplayer's career acquires darker shadings. Baseball is a hard game to play. Each day of the season is a challenge, and often the off-season is too. Every game carries the threat of a career-ending injury, and the less likely (but very real) possibility that the player will make a spectacular error or other bonehead play—the kind of miscue that can define a career.

The stresses of the day-to-day grind are evident in many players' demeanor: the short-tempered responses to innocent postgame questions, the assaults on water coolers and bat racks after a bad pitch or failed at bat, the occasional brawls with members of the opposing team or even teammates. Pressure is a constant in this profession.

Such stress is undeniable. For many players, though, even getting the opportunity to confront it involves surmounting a far-higher barrier: the one that blocks acceptance of their nationality, religion, or skin color.

From the earliest decades of the game, baseball players have been a remarkable mirror of the ethnic mix of the United States (as long as they had light skin). What's particularly fascinating is the way the mirror of baseball has reflected the tides of immigration in the nation as a whole through the decades..

In the late 1800s, baseball was dominated by Irish ballplayers. Just a glance at the era's most famous team—the Baltimore Orioles—will turn up such names as John McGraw, Hugh Jennings, Willie Keeler, Kid Gleason, Joe Kelley, Jack Doyle, and many others. In fact, as baseball historian Bill James pointed out in his *Historical Baseball Abstract* (1985), the game at the time was so dominated by Irish players "that many people, in the same stupid way that people today believe that blacks are born athletes, thought that the Irish were born baseball players."

But by early in this century, Irish names no longer dominated the box scores, and many nationalities were more strongly represented in the major leagues— just as they were in the country as a whole. There were players of German, French, Latin American, and other ancestry, including many first-generation Americans. There were even some Jewish ballplayers, and some Native American ones.

While the broad view of this pre–World War II era of baseball history seems to reveal remarkable ethnic harmony on the ball field, the close-up truth is different. If you weren't part of the majority, your heritage was an important issue indeed.

Hall of Famer Chief Bender, star pitcher with the Philadelphia Athletics during the first years of the century, was by all accounts an educated man of great

Crossing the Line

187

"Bender is a typical Indian in looks and demeanor," said Sporting Life *in 1905, making sure everyone knew where the great Philadelphia pitcher, whose name was Charles but who was always called "Chief," came from.*

dignity and reserve. He was also born of a Chippewa mother and a white father, a fact that everything from his nickname to his press coverage made abundantly clear.

Here are the first paragraphs of a complimentary article about Bender that appeared in *Sporting Life* in 1905:

It has not been a far cry from the tepee and the lodge, from the wood and the river, to the cities and the luxuries of the pale face for Albert Bender, scion of Indian chiefs and one of the greatest pitchers of America's national game.

Bender is a typical Indian in looks and demeanor, and the characteristic marks of his race are pronounced even in the habiliment of an American citizen.

This Indian is a magnificent type of the race of original Americans.

When Bender finally gets a chance to speak for himself in the article, his first words are ones that would be echoed many times in many ways four decades later, when players of all races are at last allowed to play organized baseball. "I avoid notoriety when I can," Bender tells the interviewer. "I do not want my name presented to the public as an Indian, but as a pitcher."

When Joe DiMaggio came to the Yankees in 1936, he was just one of many prominent ballplayers of Italian heritage at the time, along with Tony Lazzeri, Dolph Camilli, Ernie Lombardi, and other stars. Safety in numbers, though, went only so far, as DiMaggio discovered when he was the subject of a profile in *Life* Magazine in 1939. Then he learned the same lesson that Chief Bender had learned decades earlier: Neither brilliant play nor a dignified personality will deter those who are determined to focus on your ancestry.

Comparing DiMaggio to "other Italians," the article said that he was "well adapted to most U.S. mores. Instead of olive oil or smelly bear grease he keeps his hair slick with water. He never reeks of garlic." The rest of the article is equally kind, using such ethnic code words as "lazy" and "shiftless" to describe the Yankee slugger.

Given this coverage in the press, it's easy to imagine the treatment such players received on the ball field. Though during his career he always said that ethnic slights on the field didn't bother him, Hank Greenberg (the first Jewish baseball superstar) was more honest in his 1989 autobiography. "How the hell could you get up to home plate every day and have some son of a bitch call you a Jew bastard and a kike and a sheenie and get on your ass without feeling the pressure," he said. "If the ballplayers weren't doing it, the fans were. I used to get frustrated as hell."

Greenberg coped by learning to follow his own advice, which he expressed in a 1949 letter to the father of a Jewish boy who hoped to become a professional ballplayer: Don't let the racists stop you. "If prejudice does exist," the slugger wrote from experience, "then let it spur you on to greater achievement rather than accept it and be licked by it."

Greenberg, DiMaggio, Bender, and other players had to take such abuse—but at least they were allowed to play in the major leagues. Between the 1880s and 1947, professional ballplayers who happened to be African American did not even have this opportunity. Undoubtedly, any one of them would have gladly accepted the inevitable, brutal abuse as a worthwhile trade-off for the chance to play in the majors.

What made the color barrier especially frustrating was that these black ballplayers—who honed their skills in the Negro Leagues—did get to play against major-league stars in exhibition games. "I played against every big leaguer from Babe Ruth on down," said Hall of Famer Judy Johnson. "We played against the Philadelphia A's intact one year and we beat them five out of six games. I don't remember what year it was now, but I know Judge Landis was the commissioner and that was the year he banned all major league teams from playing intact against any of the Negro teams."

Ray Dandridge almost made it across the color line. A roommate of Willie Mays' with the Triple-A Minneapolis Millers in 1951, Dandridge was a consistent .300 hitter in the minors, easily good enough to deserve a call-up to the Giants. But he was thirty-eight in 1951, and the call never came. "The onliest thing I ever wanted was to put one foot in a major-league park, even if I only got to stay but a week," Dandridge said when he was inducted into the Hall of Fame in 1987.

Hall of Famer Pop Lloyd was in his sixties before the barrier finally fell, so he never had any illusions about crossing the color line. What consolation he could gain came from knowing that his outstanding talent helped open white eyes to the play of black ballplayers. "They say I was born forty years too soon," Lloyd said in a 1950 speech at a newly opened park named for him in his hometown of Atlantic City, New Jersey. "But I believe I was born at the right time, because I and other black stars of my era were the pioneers who paved the way for the recognition of Jackie Robinson and others of our race as major league talent."

By the time Jackie Robinson was chosen to be the first major-league black

Jackie Robinson being hit by a pitch. Who knows how many times pitchers threw at Robinson because of his color, and how many times because of his brilliant, fiery play?

ballplayer in sixty years, he was well aware that avoiding notoriety would be impossible. Even before he played a single game with the Brooklyn Dodgers' Montreal farm team, he had already drawn the attention of the public, press, and the majors' greatest stars—not all of whom were eager to see him succeed.

Perhaps the most prominent dissenter among ballplayers was Bob Feller, who wrote a newspaper article questioning Robinson's ability to hit major-league pitching. Responding to the article in a private letter to Wendell Smith, a sportswriter at the Pittsburgh *Courier* and a close confidant of Robinson's, Jackie displayed his famous self-confidence:

The one article by Bob Feller interests me very much inasmuch as I was worried more about my fielding than about my hitting. I value what Feller says because I faced him a couple of times and he is a very good pitcher, and when I read where he is one of the best if not the best pitcher in major league ball I feel confident that if it is left to my hitting I believe I will do alright. The few times I faced Feller has made me confident that the pitching I have faced in the Negro American League was as tough as any I will have to face if I stick with Montreal.

Robinson stuck—and starred—with Montreal in 1946. But, although he always remembered the kindness and lack of prejudice that he found among the fans and teammates there, the task of being a symbol for an entire people exacted a heavy toll from the start. In fact, as the 1946 season drew to an end, the strain became almost too great. "The doctor said that if I didn't lay off for awhile, I would have a complete mental and physical break-down," he told Smith.

Robinson took a few days off. When he returned to the lineup he felt better at first, but then "I got that old, tired feeling and it stayed with me all through the playoffs and the Little World Series. I didn't feel right until I got home."

The challenges Robinson faced when he took the next big step, to the Brooklyn Dodgers in 1947, have been described countless times. He freely admitted throughout his life that he would not have been able to succeed without the steadfast support of his wife, Rachel. "Rachel has been the inspiration behind everything I've attempted to do," he said in 1971, a year before his death, upon receiving *Sport* Magazine's Outstanding Athlete of the Quarter-Century Award. "She was the guiding light behind whatever success I've had."

Important too was the backing of a few players, both on the Dodgers and with opposing teams. Simple gestures—such as teammate Pee Wee Reese, a white southerner, putting his arm around Robinson's shoulders on the field—helped Robinson get through the difficult early days of his first season in the bigs.

In his 1948 autobiography, *Jackie Robinson: My Own Story*, Robinson tells of another such gesture—one that came from a man who understood some of what he was going through. While running out a grounder, Robinson was knocked down in a collision with the outstretched arm of Hank Greenberg, then finishing his career with the Pittsburgh Pirates. This was a play that could have been seen as another example of the sort of aggressive, borderline treatment Robinson often had to face. But the truth was far different:

Larry Doby returns in glory to his alma mater, Eastside High School in Paterson, New Jersey, after his superb 1948 season with Cleveland. "I was, sort of, the school hero," he recalled of his years at Eastside, "always one of the crowd, going everywhere with my white schoolmates, parties, dances, shows."

The next inning Hank came to bat and got a walk. When he got to first base, he said, "Did I hurt you on that play last inning, Jackie?"

"No, Hank," I answered, "I'm okay."

"I was stretching to get the ball," he said. "I didn't mean to knock you down."

"That's all right," I assured him. "I tried to get out of your way too, but I couldn't."

The big handsome Pirate slugger smiled and said, "Listen, don't pay any attention to these guys who are trying to make it hard for you. Stick in there. You're doing fine. The next time you come to Pittsburgh, I hope you and I can get together for a talk. There are a few things I've learned through the years that might help you and make it easier."

I thanked him from the bottom of my heart. Those words of encouragement helped me tremendously. I knew that he was sincere because I had heard he had [as a Jew] experienced some racial trouble when he came up. I felt sure that he understood my problems. I liked him, too. That man had class, Hank Greenberg did.

For Larry Doby, the first African American to play in the American League, it was Jackie Robinson who helped, as he told the *Los Angeles Times* in 1974.

I'd call him late at night, and Jackie and I agreed we shouldn't challenge anybody or cause trouble—or we'd both be out of the big leagues, just like that.

We figured that if we spoke out, we would ruin things for other black players. The time wasn't right for that in those days. We didn't want to do anything that would keep guys like Willie Mays and Henry Aaron from coming along later.

Jackie and I talked often . . . maybe we kept each other from giving up.

Larry Doby, sliding home and illustrating the aggressive baserunning that characterized his play in the early years of baseball integration.

Monte Irvin didn't make it to the majors until he was thirty years old. "I sincerely believe that if I'd been able to play big league ball right from the start, I could've set some batting records comparable to DiMaggio, Mays, Aaron, Williams—six or seven hundred home runs, that type of thing," Irvin said.

Unlike Ray Dandridge, Monte Irvin was just young enough to figure in the Giants' future once Robinson and Doby had blazed the trail. But he couldn't avoid thinking about what might have been, especially upon being inducted into the Hall of Fame in a special 1973 election for Negro League players. "I'm philosophical about it," he said then about the fact that he had to wait until he was thirty before making it to the majors. "I was way past my peak then. My only regret was that I didn't get a shot at 19, when I was a real ballplayer."

Robinson, Doby, and the American black ballplayers who followed them weren't the only ones to benefit from the relaxation of the color line. While there had been a few Latin ballplayers in the majors (beginning in 1914, Cuban-born Dolf Luque pitched for twenty years in the majors, for example), the 1950s saw the beginning of an influx of Latin stars from the Dominican Republic, Cuba, Puerto Rico, and elsewhere.

The road these stars had to travel was not easy either. They were often far from home, having to learn a new language quickly, in a country whose mores and codes of conduct were alien to their own experience. No wonder loneliness struck many of them hard.

When he first came from the Dominican Republic to play with the Giants' farm team in Michigan City, Michigan, Hall of Fame pitcher Juan Marichal was extremely homesick, as he told the *Boston Globe* in 1974:

I'd brought some records with me from the Dominican. Oh, I guess you can call them boleros. Very sentimental records.

I'd play them every night. I'd come home and I'd play those records. Every night. And I'd feel worse and worse.

Then one day I started to think about why I was in this game, that I was here to better my economic situation. What was I going to do if I went home to the few heads of cattle and goats? That's where I'd be for the rest of my life and I'd never have another chance.

I took those records out and I destroyed them.

Loneliness was not the exclusive province of rookies. "The day I get off the plane from Venezuela, I want to get back on it and go back," said Luis Aparicio upon arriving at spring training in 1965, his tenth season. "Baseball is my business but it is harder and harder to stay away from my family."

The great Roberto Clemente, who was born in Puerto Rico, had perhaps the

Juan Marichal always seemed supremely self-confident on the mound, but the native of the Dominican Republic was often lonely in his early years with the Giants.

most clear-eyed view of the obstacles facing Latin ballplayers, as he showed in this 1964 *Sporting News* interview:

I've heard American scouts tell me about Latin players they have signed and, when they see these kids in the United States, they can't believe it's the same boy.

Maybe this is puzzling to Americans, but it isn't puzzling to any of us from Latin America or Cuba who have gone through this ordeal.

It takes all of us some time to get adjusted.

We lead different lives in America. We're always meeting new people, seeing new faces. The language barrier is great at first and we have trouble ordering food in restaurants. Even segregation baffles us.

It takes time for us to settle down emotionally. Once we're at peace with the world, we can do the job in baseball. The people who have never experienced these problems don't know what it's like.

Tom Seaver struggled with his composure at a farewell press conference in New York, after he was traded by the Mets to Cincinnati on June 15, 1977. When emotion kept him from speaking, Seaver wrote his thoughts down, referring to the fan reaction to his passing Sandy Koufax in the all-time strikeout list.

And The ovation the other night after passing S Koufax will be one of the most memorable and warm moments in my life.

Moving On

Fans tend to look at baseball trades as a matter of profit and loss: Did our team gain more than it gave up? For players, though, being traded can be a shattering experience, leaving behind a bitter sense of rejection that can take years to fade.

"To say I was dumbfounded is to put it mildly," Eddie Collins said of hearing he'd been traded from Philadelphia to the Chicago White Sox before the 1915 season. "I felt as if I had been sandbagged. My knees turned to jelly and queer convulsions rumbled through my innards."

Collins went on to say that, once he got used to the idea, some of the happiest days of his life were those he spent with the White Sox. But he was far from alone in feeling as if the earth had suddenly shifted under his feet and might never be steady again.

Often, the traded player finds himself thrown onto a team that, until then, had been a bitter enemy. Jackie Robinson wouldn't do it; he retired rather than leave the Dodgers for the archrival Giants in 1957. Frankie Frisch decided to see it through when, after spending eight seasons with John McGraw's rough-riding Giants, he found himself on his way to the St. Louis Cardinals.

"Baseball was rent by as many feuds as the Kentucky hills of the Hatfields and the McCoys," Frisch recalled of those days. "When I was traded to the Cardinals in 1926, no one spoke to me for a week. In the eyes of St. Louis, I was still one of McGraw's hated Giants, a dead-end kid with brass knuckles on my fists."

For many players, the shock of being traded is intensified by the effect it has on their uprooted families. At the best of times, a baseball career—requiring, as it does, intense self-absorption and months spent away from wife and children each year—can be extremely hard on a player's home life. Being sent to a new city just makes the challenges even greater.

When Orlando Cepeda was traded from the Cardinals to the Braves in 1969, his first thoughts were for his young son. "He knows something has happened," Cepeda said of three-year-old Orlandito, "but he doesn't know what yet. It's going to be strange to him when he sees me in the other uniform."

Then Cepeda went on to speak for himself and his wife, Ana. "This club here, we have so many friends," he said of the Cardinals. "We have such happiness in St. Louis, but what can you do?"

Hall of Fame third baseman George Kell had already been traded twice in his career when he was sent from the Red Sox to the White Sox during the 1954 season. But this trade seemed to hurt the worst. "The toughest part of the whole thing is to have to call my wife and tell her," Kell told reporters upon hearing the news. "She loved it in Boston. She'll be really hurt."

Then Kell (who would be dealt once more before his career ended) spoke words that showed clearly how hurt he'd been by the trade. "Baseball is no game for a family man," he said. "I hope my boy never gets to play baseball as a professional."

Playing in Pain

The aches and pains that are the ballplayer's natural lot have afflicted the game's participants since the earliest days of its history. As early as 1867, the pioneering baseball writer and promoter Henry Chadwick was publishing *The Ball Players' Chronicle*, which at least once focused on the perils of the national game. Here's the conclusion of a report by one "Brick Pomeroy" on his experiences upon joining a ball club:

That was an eventful chap who first invented base ball. It's such fun. I've played five games, and this is the result:

> *Twenty-seven dollars paid out for things.*
> *One bunged eye—badly bunged.*
> *One broken little finger.*
> *One bump on the head.*
> *Nineteen lame backs.*
> *One sore jaw.*
> *One thumb dislocated.*
> *Three sprained ankles.*
> *Five swelled legs.*
> *One dislocated shoulder from trying to throw the ball a thousand yards.*
> *Two hands raw from trying to stop hot balls.*
> *A lump the size of a hornet's nest on left hip, well back.*
> *A nose sweetly jammed, and five uniforms spoiled from rolling in the dirt at the bases.*
> *I have played two weeks, and don't think I like the game.*

This piece was intended to be humorous. Yet it would prove to be all too accurate for many players down through baseball's history. Basically, any game that makes such unpredictable demands on its athletes must take a toll, one that is barely recognized by the average fan.

Sometimes the toll is unavoidable—the result of too much pounding of the legs, too many throws, just one too many unnatural movements by a body not designed for the stresses of baseball.

In 1948, for example, Joe DiMaggio suffered terribly from bone spurs in his right heel—enduring a pain he compared to biting pennies with a toothache; it forced him to walk to the clubhouse on tiptoes after some games. Despite surgery to remove the bone spurs, DiMaggio found that he was still in pain as the 1949 season began. The realization that he might never fully recover, and that his career might be in jeopardy, led the normally polite and reserved Yankee to lash out at the press for their incessant questions about his condition: "You guys are driving me batty. Can't you leave me alone?" he said. "This affects me mentally too, you know."

Well, the Yankees did make the Series, and won it easily against the Dodgers, but a pain-racked DiMaggio managed to hit only .118.

Forty years later, another Yankee star, Don Mattingly, was going through similar torment. Early in his career, Mattingly appeared to be building a case for undeniable Hall of Fame qualifications. Each season from 1984 to 1986, for example, he hit between .324 and .352, got more than 200 hits, led the league in doubles, and drove in more than 100 runs.

Then his back began to protest, and his batting average and productivity plummeted. Mattingly never blamed his injury for his dwindling statistics, but on August 30, 1997, when his number was retired at Yankee Stadium, he described what he'd gone through. "I was born with a congenital defect," he said. "If I hit too much, I got a pounding soreness. It was like a dead ache in my back."

Many players struggle through entire seasons—even great parts of their careers—in pain. The Mets' star catcher Gary Carter described his damaged right knee as the 1985 season drew to a close: "I feel it just about every minute of the day," he told the *New York Post* that September. "I feel it when I'm walking, or even lying in bed. Really, there are days when I wake up, and I try to roll over and I hear the thing cracking. That hurts."

To keep his season going, Carter resorted to babying the knee as much as possible. "When we're home, I spend most of the day in the house. There's no sense moving around," he explained. "Same thing on the road. I stay in the hotel, order room service. Avoid walking. I'm smart enough to know not to go shopping. And if I'm going to walk, I stop every couple of blocks."

This was a thirty-one-year-old man talking.

Sometimes, injuries are inexplicable—but that doesn't make them any less debilitating. Toward the end of his career, Hall of Famer Johnny Evers suffered one such affliction, as he told *Baseball Magazine* in 1917:

Once I considered baseball as a sport and later as a profession. It is both. Sometimes I think a man has to be a philosopher not to consider it a tragedy—or a joke. If I was a pitcher I might expect, after my long term in the game, to have trouble with my arm. I would take it as a matter of course. But I am not a pitcher. Even as an infielder I could understand trouble with my throwing arm. But it is not my throwing arm which bothers me. It is my left arm which I never use for anything save in fielding the ball and in holding the bat. Why should I have trouble with my left arm which I use so little? It is one of baseball's little jokes and I guess the joke is on me.

While the sort of injuries suffered by DiMaggio, Mattingly, Evers, and countless other stars over the years are acknowledged as a logical price to pay for a long baseball career, it is the threat of a freak injury that gives ballplayers nightmares. The bad hop that sends a ball into a unprotected bare hand, the seam in the artificial turf that catches the spikes and tears up a knee, the pitched ball hurtling toward the batter's head at ninety-five miles per hour—these can end even the greatest career in an instant.

Yet what can a player do? There's really no choice but to be philosophical about the possibility of disaster. Sunny Jim Bottomley, a Hall of Fame first baseman with the Cardinals, for example, treated being the target of a Babe Ruth line drive as he might discuss being in the path of a tornado. The following is from a *Baseball Magazine* article in 1927:

I caught one off Babe myself in spring training this year. I heard the bat crack the ball. I got a glimpse of a white streak coming straight. I reached out my gloved hand, but the ball was a sinker. It dove two feet. I had just time to

Opposite, above:
Roberto Clemente playing in pain, as he did during so much of his career.

Opposite, below:
Joe DiMaggio, bedeviled throughout much of his career by leg and knee injuries: "Sooner or later, as you get up in the thirties, your legs are going to go back on you," DiMaggio lamented.

198

put my hand down close to my leg and stop the ball. But that hand was numb for three days. If Babe ever hit them through the pitcher's box instead of pulling them to right field, there'd be a lot of pitchers ruined in the American League.

True, and that applied to other hitters and pitchers as well. On opening night of the season for a minor-league team in Birmingham, Alabama, reliever Rollie Fingers was pitching when an opposing hitter smashed a ball up the middle. "I saw it about three feet from my face," Fingers told *The Sporting News* two years later. "I knew it was coming up the middle from the moment he hit it. I threw up my arms in front of my face. But it came through my arms."

The ball broke Fingers' jaw and shattered his cheekbone, but the pitcher recovered, joined the Oakland A's relief corps in 1969, and helped lead the team to three consecutive World Championships (1972–74) in the course of a seventeen-year Hall of Fame career.

Earle Combs, an outfielder for the Yankees during the dynasty years of the 1920s and 1930s, suffered three major injuries during his career, including a broken leg and broken arm. Then, in July 1934, chasing a long fly by the St. Louis Browns' Harlond Clift, the future Hall of Famer crashed into the right-field wall of St. Louis's Sportsman's Park.

Forty-one-year-old Johnny Evers in 1922, seeing a future without baseball.

"I could see the ball sailing over my head and I knew that all that was needed was a little jump," Combs said from his hospital bed, where he was recovering from a broken shoulder and head injuries. "I leaped and got the ball, but crashed into the wall just as I made the catch. That was all I knew until I woke up in the clubhouse. My shoulder hurt badly and while I could see, everything appeared double."

Combs never made it all the way back from his injury, playing only a part of one more season before retiring. Still, he did recover his health, something that cannot be said for some victims of one of the most frightening occurrences in baseball: being hit in the head by a pitched ball.

The most famous instance, of course, is the beaning of Ray Chapman by submarine pitcher Carl Mays in 1920, which resulted in Chapman's death. While no other major leaguer has been killed by a pitched ball since then, many other players have been seriously hurt. Even batting helmets, worn routinely since the 1950s, cannot guarantee protection.

In 1967, Tony Conigliaro, a rising star with the Boston Red Sox, stepped into the batter's box in the fourth inning of a home game against Jack Hamilton of the Los Angeles Angels. In his 1970 autobiography, *Seeing it Through*, Conigliaro described what happened next:

The ball came sailing right toward my chin. Normally, a hitter can just jerk his head back a fraction and the ball will buzz right by. But this pitch seemed to follow me in. I know I didn't freeze, I definitely made a move to get out of the way of the ball. In fact, I jerked my head back so hard that my helmet flipped off just before impact.

Funny, you never go up there thinking you're going to be hit, and then in a fraction of a second you know it's going to happen. When the ball was about four feet from my head I knew it was going to get me. And I knew it was going to hurt because Hamilton was such a hard thrower. I was frightened. I threw my hands up in front of my face and saw the ball follow me back and hit me square in the left side of the head. As soon as it crunched into me, it felt as if the ball would go in my head and come out the other side; my legs gave way and I went down like a sack of potatoes. Just before everything went dark I saw the ball bounce straight down on home plate. It was the last thing I saw for several days.

I was never knocked out but I wish I had been. I rolled on the ground trying to stop the pain in my head with my hands. The impact of the ball made both my eyes slam shut and I felt a tremendous swelling in my mouth. I couldn't see. I remember saying I'm blind, I can't see, *I remember saying that.*

The full story of the extent of Conigliaro's injury—his doctors thought he might die from bleeding around his brain—and his long, slow recovery from double vision and other effects of the beaning makes for harrowing reading. It's a testament to his courage and determination that he worked his way back to the majors, even hitting 36 home runs in 1970. But then his vision went bad again, and his career stumbled to a close by 1971 (when he was just twenty-six years old), not counting a brief attempted comeback in 1975.

Being the Goat

Of course, most great players don't suffer the fate of a Tony Conigliaro, or even the repeated serious injuries of an Earle Combs. But there isn't a player alive—not Ty Cobb, not Ted Williams, nobody—who hasn't suffered through another type of baseball misery: the agonizing slump.

Even the greatest stars feel uncertain, naked even, when they suddenly seem to lose the abilities they've come to depend on. They can't believe it's happening to them; they don't know why it's happening at all. They get angry at themselves and at others. They ask for advice—or angrily reject helpful suggestions when offered. They study films of their pitching motions or batting stances, seeking even the slightest clue as to why their fastball is staying up in the strike zone or why they're missing pitches they should slam for home runs. They agonize . . . until, one day, usually for inexplicable reasons, they just get back on track.

In his 1979 autobiography, *Catch You Later*, Reds' Hall of Famer Johnny Bench describes the frustration of being in a season-long batting slump (as he was in 1971). He begins by saying that, though pitchers always focus intensely on the opposing team's best players, great hitters can overcome this by being selective and careful at the plate:

Instead, I was worrying and developing bad habits. I'd pull away from the ball in my stride, take pitches on the outside corner I couldn't believe were strikes, then swing at them when I knew I couldn't reach them. And the more dumb things I did, the more I buried myself.

It's next to impossible to explain the pressure of professional sports. And the concentration needed to meet it. The reason for a lot of failure of 1971 lay somewhere in my concentration, when I had it, when I lost it, and to what degree. The equilibrium you need to do the job vanished so quickly, and I went through periods when I didn't know which way to turn.

I tried everything: changed my helmets, bats, grips, stances, chewing tobacco. I tried to figure out what I was doing when I was going good. I looked at movies, photographs, and oil paintings. But baseball is filled with variables. I may have been doing everything right, then guess fastball, get a breaking pitch, and pop it up. Then it seemed that nothing matched up. If I started worrying about one thing, then something else went out.

Rogers Hornsby took a different tack when he was slumping—and yes, even a man with a lifetime batting average of .358 went through bleak periods. Here's Hornsby in *Baseball Magazine* in 1920:

I cannot explain slumps. If I could explain them and what is better, outline a quick cure for them, I would not have to play baseball for a living. I could earn much more by coaching other batters.

All that you can say of slumps is that they come to everyone regardless of his ability and go in time, if your patience holds out or the manager doesn't can you before you get into your stride once more. There are batters who study themselves continually when they are in a slump. They analyze their mental feelings and the way they hold the bat and the way they shuffle their feet, in fact everything they do. And they try out new stunts in an effort to

"When I slump, I really slump," said
Johnny Bench of his 1971 season, when
he hit a mere .238.

Rogers Hornsby's prescription for avoiding slumps: "Get a good ball to hit!"

discover the winning combination. This may be all well enough. But to me it seems like poor dope. For the man who studies himself in a batting slump is of necessity, keeping his mind on his troubles. And usually trouble doesn't become any less, the more you dwell on it.

When the unwelcome knowledge breaks in on me that I am off my batting stride I go to some wise batter on our club and tell him to look me over and try to find what is wrong. Then I endeavor to think about something else. In time he will come to me and suggest that I try not to swing quite so soon when I meet the ball, or stand a little closer to the plate, or some simple thing which he believes would help me. I give his suggestion a workout and before long discover that I am stinging them as hard as ever.

If Hornsby not only makes sense, but even sounds sanguine about what is needed to get out of a slump, it should be noted that he gave this interview during a season in which he led the league with a .370 batting average. So perhaps it was easy for him to sound calm and reasonable.

In truth, anyone who has heard of Hornsby's legendary temper knows that he must have been a hard man to be around when things weren't going so well.

And he wasn't the only one. When any superstar is gripped by this sort of slump, it may be best for everyone around him to tread lightly.

During a difficult stretch for Willie Mays in 1957, for example, Giants Manager Bill Rigney would have been well advised to avoid Mays entirely instead of offering tips during batting practice. "It doesn't help to stand behind that cage and make remarks because that's the time to leave me alone," Mays griped at the time. "I'm trying to time my swing with that pitcher and I can't listen to somebody talking about my feet. This slumping is nothing new, and I always get out of it by myself."

By the way, Mays hit .333 in 1957, so *something* got him out of his slump. But six years later, after suffering through an 0–18 drought at the plate, Mays sounded sad and defensive at suggestions that—at age thirty-two—he was on the downside of his career. "Here we go again," he said. "It just seems some guys wait until me or somebody else goes bad and they knock us down and kick us. Believe me, nobody knows better than me that my batting average is low. I sleep with it."

Mays wasn't the only one to bring poor play home with him. "I think I dream about baseball almost every night," said Luis Aparicio when he was struggling. "I dream I make a real bad job. You always wake up in the best part, the worst part. You know, in dreams, you make an error, you wake up."

Then there's always denial. In a 1910 interview, Hall of Famer Napoleon Lajoie (nicknamed "Larry") simply refused to acknowledge that slumps exist:

There is no such thing as a batting slump. It's just the luck of the game— that's all. Here is the way it goes: I go up and hit the ball. The fielder goes after it. He just gets it. I am out. Back to the bench for me. I go up again. Hit the ball hard. Same thing. I go up again and hit the ball. That man out in center goes crazy with the heat. Runs three miles, jumps twelve feet in the air and catches it on his thumb. I get that handed to me for three or four days, and the people begin to say: "What's the matter with Larry? Not a hit in three days." Now, I am hitting that ball just as hard as ever, but the luck of the game is against me; that's all. The next day I go up and swat it, and some guy in the field runs under it too far, and I get around to second, and some fans say, "Well, Larry is getting his batting eye back again." Then, again. The bases are filled. I walk up to the plate. I get my eye on the ball and paste it hard. It sails out on a line, and the infielder who goes after it finds his arm half an inch too short. The ball keeps rolling, and two or three runs come in, and Larry gets credit for it all. Great batter! Now, if that infielder had not stood quite so close to himself, and had grown half an inch more of arm, the side would have been retired, and everybody would have said, "See, the old bonehead hit right into someone's hands." That's baseball for you. It's the luck of the game.

Sometimes, for inexplicable reasons, a slump stretches on beyond typical boundaries, and the struggling player joins the fans in wondering if his skills have vanished for good. Rube Marquard, star pitcher with the Giants and other teams early in this century, found that his extended slump came at the worst possible time: In 1909 and 1910, during his first two full years in the majors.

Exacerbating his problems was the fact that his struggles came after a sparkling stint in the minors that led to his signing with the Giants for $11,000—a large sum at the time for an unproven pitcher.

Still, regardless of the details, Marquard's passionate description—which appeared under the title of "How It Seems to Be a Big League Failure" in a 1912 issue of *Baseball Magazine*—could describe the self-doubts that must creep into the minds of even the most confident of baseball stars:

For two years or more I was called the great $11,000 "lemon." The spectators used to shout it at me from the bleachers; the press used to print it in big letters; I saw or heard it everywhere. The lot of the average bench warmer is a hard one, but the lot of the young player who has brought a big price and who is naturally expected to deliver gilt-edged ball is particularly unpleasant. . . .

I shall never forget my first game in big league company. It is still so vivid in my mind that I cannot look back on it now with any degree of comfort. We were playing Cincinnati. The people turned out in great crowds to see the new "phenom" pitch. The records said that there were 30,000 people present, but when I entered the pitcher's box, with my knees knocking together, and looked up into the stands, I could see at least double that number. I was only eighteen at the time and extremely anxious to make good, but I had small hopes of living up to the high expectations of my work which the crowd seemed to entertain, and I was extremely nervous. The mere fact that I was so anxious to make good made it impossible for me to do myself justice. I could not bear to think what the crowd might say if I should hit a batter in my nervousness, and in an effort to avoid this I was extremely wild. Then when I tried to gain control by putting them over the plate, I had to depend solely on a straight ball, which I was not able to handle with my ordinary good luck. Then the balls started coming for me like rifle shots and went as safe hits. It was a slaughter and I blew up completely. . . .

That was the only game I took part in that season, but it was enough. I was so badly rattled that I did not get over it all winter. The opening of the next season found me in fully as bad condition, or worse.

I lost confidence completely, and the knocks which the press and the spectators gave me did not help matters any. When I was pitching, the moment I failed to put them over, there would be a series of calls, "Take him out" and various comments on the $11,000 "lemon." Criticism of this kind is very unnerving to a young player new to the game. It gets the nerves of the old timers, too, to some extent, but they are more used to it and can stand it better. Still, where many thousands of voices are shouting at once "Take him out," the pitcher is likely to grow discouraged, and I do not believe any man can do his best under such circumstances. . . .

This thing went on for more than two years, until last spring I made up my mind I would either make good or get out of the game.

Remarkably, Marquard did make good: His record in his third full season was a sparkling 24–7. This was followed by 26–11, 23–10, and a career that landed him in the Hall of Fame. Still, the pain and self-doubt that infused that interview stand as a testament to the intense challenges of this hard game.

If there's one characteristic shared by all the finest players in baseball history, it's their ability to overcome loneliness, slumps, injuries, and the other pressures exerted both from within themselves and without. But the one hurdle that none can forestall forever, of course, is the end of the career.

Most players who are facing the end are remarkably philosophical: They've seen time work its inevitable effects on the stars who preceded them, and realize that—at an age that someone in almost any other profession would still be considered a young man—they too will soon have to surrender the spotlight.

In some cases, this realization comes well before the curtain falls, especially when a serious injury threatens to short-circuit a rising career. In 1962, just a year after he finally became a dominating pitcher, Sandy Koufax suffered a mysterious finger injury that ended his season prematurely. "All last winter, while my finger was healing, I didn't know if my career was over or not," he told *Sports Illustrated* in 1963, and then went on:

And there are other things to think about. Sometimes it seems like a dream world. It seems like I should have everything a man could want now, but who knows what's gonna happen. When is it gonna end? I feel that if I could play till I'm 40 or 38 or 36 and be successful till then, sure, then I would have everything I want. But if it's over next year, what have I got? The money I've made I could spend in a very short time. I have some schooling, but I'm not really prepared to do anything except pitch. The thought is always there that it might end quickly. I remember too many great arms, too many pitchers that everybody thought were going to be great, and all of a sudden it was over.

Sandy Koufax was only thirty when he was forced to retire. He knew how precious and fragile a baseball career is.

Koufax did bounce back from that finger injury, but his career was cut short by another injury, the arthritic elbow that forced him from the game at age thirty, at the very height of his powers. Unlike those other pitchers he mentioned, though, at least Koufax was given the chance to prove his greatness, and did so as brilliantly as any pitcher in the game's history.

Most players, however, don't discuss the end of their careers until they begin to feel their age and declining skills. For some, the approaching finale brings only resentment and denial. How could it not, in individuals who have already overcome so many hurdles and still feel strong and vigorous inside? Cy Young's reaction was typical: "When I quit the Boston Club in Pittsburgh it was because I was not in shape to pitch," Young said in 1912. "But I am not broken down by any means. I am still better than three-fourths of the pitchers in the league."

Perhaps he really believed that, but his age (forty-four) and his arm—which had thrown a mind-boggling 7,356 innings in the major leagues—told a different story. "After I rest awhile I am going to get a country kid who can catch me and see if I have control. . . . Don't think I am through yet," Young insisted. But he never pitched in the majors again.

Of course, many of these brave words may have been for public consumption. On the inside, ballplayers are the first to know when their skills are eroding. "A ballplayer can feel it coming. Pitchers I used to own now overpower me," said Hall of Famer Charlie Gehringer. Joe Sewell agreed, saying, "You know, there isn't anybody on earth who knows better than yourself that you've slowed up, but you don't tell that to anybody."

At the very end, players can be brutally honest with themselves. "I think I'm too young to be considered through as a major league pitcher," said Hal Newhouser in 1953. "But I can't kid myself." Grover Cleveland Alexander also conceded to reality after being released by the Phillies in 1930: "I'm afraid I'm through as a big-league pitcher. It's like the one-horse shay, you know, it doesn't last forever."

Sadly, even some of the most self-aware stars find it hard to stay away from the game that has been central to their lives for so long. "I owe Chicago a great deal, but I don't feel that I owe baseball or the great Chicago public my life," said the Cubs' star first baseman Frank Chance, upon announcing his retirement in 1911 after suffering concussions from being beaned. But Chance, like so many others, reneged on his retirement, attempting several brief and unsuccessful comebacks.

In 1962, at the age of forty-one, the Cards' Stan Musial hit a stunning .330. Some suggested he retire on this high note, but he chose to play one more year. "I had the thrill of going through an exciting pennant race, one that just failed to produce the greatest stretch drive of all," he wrote of the 1963 season, in which he hit .255. "And I had the satisfaction of reaching that point where, without anyone else having to tell me, I realized my liabilities were about to outweigh my assets as a ball player."

After that valedictory year, Musial, modest and clear-eyed as always, resisted any temptation to tack on yet another "final year," and bowed out gracefully.

As did Mike Schmidt, who retired midseason in 1989 rather than harm the team (and his own legacy) by struggling on. "I gave it some time to turn around

"I tried to win, but I couldn't," Grover Cleveland Alexander (left) said upon leaving the majors in 1930. But that didn't keep him from making a "comeback" with the House of David barnstorming team the next year. He violated training rules by getting a shave and a haircut before spring training.

Opposite:
Stan Musial after his final game, September 30, 1963. He said, "I knew I would miss the action, the excitement, the thrill of putting on the uniform, the competition, the travel, the fuss of the fans, and . . ."

on the field," he said in his retirement news conference. "I looked for signs and reasons every night to continue as a player but I just couldn't find them.

"You may not be able to tell," Schmidt continued, "but this is a joyous time for me. I've had a great career." This sentiment—the sense of relief that he had conquered the hard game and no longer had anything left to prove—has been shared by baseball stars since the game's beginnings.

Carl Yastrzemski, for example, felt as if he had shed a great burden. "I loved the game, I loved the competition, but I never enjoyed it," he told reporters after his final game with the Red Sox. "It was all hard work, all the time."

Ty Cobb agreed. "I thought I would miss it a lot more, but I haven't," he told an interviewer, after a year away from the game. "It's a great old game, but I've almost felt like a prisoner who was set free. Baseball was to me more work than play . . . in fact, it was all work. You see, I was lucky enough to lead the league when I was twenty years old. After that I wanted to lead it every year. I never thought I was any genius, so I gave up my life to the game for twenty-five years."

Hall of Fame shortstop Rabbit Maranville knew exactly what Cobb was talking about. In a 1936 article in *American Legion Monthly* (written soon after his final season), Maranville reviewed his own long career—and provided a fitting conclusion to the autobiography of baseball:

For a quarter century I've been playing baseball for pay. It has been pretty good pay, most of the time. The work has been hard, but what of it? It's been risky. I've broken both my legs. I've sprained everything I've got between my ankles and my disposition. I've dislocated my joints and I've fractured my pride. I've spent more time in hospitals than some fellows ever spend in church. I've ridden on railroad trains until a steam shovel couldn't lift the cinders I've combed out of my hair. I've eaten lousy food and slept on literally lousy beds. I've been socked with fists and pop bottles and insults. I've been broken out of bed in the middle of the night by fat-headed bums who only wanted to know what Pop Anson's all-time batting average was. I've lost a lot of teeth and square yards of hide. But I've never lost my self-respect, and I've kept what I find in few men of my age—my enthusiasm. And I don't just mean my enthusiasm for baseball, though that continues even in the hot stove season.

If I had my life to live all over again do you know what I'd do? I'd be a big-league baseball player, that's what I'd do.

bibliography

Over the decades, dozens of baseball players have told their life stories. The books below include those I used in compiling *The Autobiography of Baseball*, as well as other notable player autobiographies. In addition, I've listed a handful of non-autobiographical works—such as G. H. Fleming's *The Unforgettable Season* and Bill James' *Historical Baseball Abstract*—because they paint such indelible pictures of the personalities of the great figures in baseball history.

Many of the most surprising and insightful glances at the life of a ballplayer can be found in newspapers and magazines. For more than a hundred years, *The Sporting News* has given players the chance to speak for themselves, and for the first half of this century, *Baseball Magazine* did the same. *Sporting Life*, *Baseball Digest*, *USA Today's Baseball Weekly*, *Sports Illustrated*, *Sport*, *Inside Sports*, *Collier's*, *The Saturday Evening Post*, *The New York Times*, *The Washington Post*, *The Los Angeles Times*, and many other periodicals were also valuable resources.

Ken Smith, past director of the Hall of Fame, spent every spring training for many years in the 1960s and 1970s visiting teams during spring training and interviewing players and ex-players. I relied on his thoughtful interviews for several of the excerpts in this book. I am equally grateful to interviewer Walter Langford, who caught up with Carl Hubbell, Joe Sewell, Travis Jackson, and other former superstars and got them to tell wonderful stories about baseball in the olden days.

Aaron, Hank, with Lonnie Wheeler. *I Had a Hammer*. New York: Harper Collins, 1991.

Aaron, Henry, with Furman Bisher. *Aaron*. New York: Thomas Y. Crowell, 1974.

Alvarez, Mark, ed. *The Perfect Game*. Dallas: Taylor, 1993.

Bench, Johnny, and William Brashler. *Catch You Later*. New York: Harper and Row, 1979.

Berra, Yogi, and Ed Fitzgerald. *Yogi*. Garden City, N.Y.: Doubleday, 1961.

Cairns, Bob. *Pen Men*. New York: St. Martin's, 1992.

Carew, Rod, with Ira Berkow. *Carew*. New York: Simon and Schuster, 1979.

Opposite:
Slick-fielding Lou Boudreau, hanging on to force Joe DiMaggio at second.

Carey, Max. *How to Play the Outfield and How to Steal Bases.* Plymouth, N.H.: Draper-Maynard, 1920.

Carmichael, John P., as told to. *My Greatest Day in Baseball.* New York: Grosset & Dunlap, 1951.

Charnley, Mitchell V., ed. *Secrets of Baseball told by Big League Players.* New York: D. Appleton and Company, 1927.

Conigliaro, Tony, with Jack Zanger. *Seeing It Through.* New York: Macmillan, 1970.

Connor, Anthony J. *Baseball for the Love of It.* New York: Macmillan, 1982.

Feller, Bob. *How to Pitch.* New York: A.S. Barnes, 1948.

Fleming, G. H. *The Unforgettable Season.* New York: Penguin, 1981.

Ford, Whitey, Mickey Mantle, and Joseph Durso. *Whitey and Mickey.* New York: Viking, 1977.

Foster, John B., ed. *How to Pitch.* New York: American Sports Publishing, 1908.

Gibson, Bob, with Phil Pepe. *From Ghetto to Glory: The Story of Bob Gibson.* New York: Prentice-Hall, 1968.

Greenberg, Hank, ed. by Ira Berkow. *Hank Greenberg: The Story of My Life.* New York: Times Books, 1989.

Hernandez, Keith, and Mike Bryan. *Pure Baseball.* New York: HarperCollins, 1994.

Howe, Irwin M., ed. *Pitching Course.* Chicago: Baseball Correspondence League of America, 1912.

Jackson, Reggie, with Mike Lupica. *Reggie: The Autobiography.* New York: Villard, 1984.

James, Bill. *The Bill James Guide to Baseball Managers.* New York: Scribner, 1997.

———. *The Bill James Historical Baseball Abstract.* New York: Villard, 1986.

Keller, Richard. *Orlando Cepeda: The Baby Bull.* San Francisco: Woodford Publishing, 1987.

Koufax, Sandy, with Ed Linn. *Koufax.* New York: Viking, 1966.

Lane, F. C. *Batting.* New York: Baseball Magazine Co., 1925.

Mantle, Mickey. *The Education of a Baseball Player.* New York: Simon and Schuster, 1967.

Marichal, Juan, with Charles Einstein. *A Pitcher's Story.* Garden City, N.Y.: Doubleday, 1967.

Mays, Willie, as told to Charles Einstein. *Born to Play Ball.* New York: Putnam, 1955.

Musial, Stan, as told to Bob Broeg. *Stan Musial: The Man's Own Story.* Garden City, N.Y.: Doubleday, 1964.

Paige, Leroy Satchel, as told to Hal Lebovitz. *Pitchin' Man: Satchel Paige's Own Story.* Westport, Conn.: Meckler, 1992.

Palmer, Jim, ed. by Joel H. Cohen. *Pitching.* New York: Atheneum, 1975.

Ripken, Cal, Jr., and Mike Bryan. *The Only Way I Know.* New York: Viking, 1997.

Ritter, Lawrence, ed. *The Glory of Their Times.* New York: Macmillan, 1966.

Robinson, Frank, and Berry Stainback. *Extra Innings.* New York: McGraw-Hill, 1988.

Robinson, Frank, with Al Silverman. *My Life Is Baseball*. Garden City, N.Y.: Doubleday, 1968.

Robinson, Jackie, as told to Wendell Smith. *My Own Story*. New York: Greenberg: Publisher, 1948.

Robinson, Jackie, ed. by Charles Dexter. *Baseball Has Done It*. Philadelphia: Lippincott, 1964.

Rowan, Carl T., with Jackie Robinson. *Wait Till Next Year*. New York: Random House, 1960.

Ryan, Nolan, with Jerry Jenkins. *Miracle Man*. Dallas: Word Publishing, 1992.

Schiffer, Don, ed. *My Greatest Baseball Game*. New York: A.S. Barnes, 1950.

Seaver, Tom, with Lee Lowenfish. *The Art of Pitching*. New York: Mountain Lion/Hearst Books, 1984.

Williams, Billy, and Irv Haag. *Billy: The Classic Hitter*. New York: Rand McNally, 1974.

Williams, Ted, and John Underwood. *The Science of Hitting*. New York: Simon and Schuster, 1968.

Williams, Ted, with John Underwood. *My Turn at Bat: The Story of My Life*. New York: Simon and Schuster, 1969.

Wray, J. E., ed. *How to Play First Base*. New York: American Sports Publishing, 1907.

——. *How to Play Second Base*. New York: American Sports Publishing, 1905.

——. *How to Play Third Base*. New York: American Sports Publishing, 1909.

——. *How to Run the Bases*. New York: American Sports Publishing, 1908.

index

photograph credits